BRUCE
MARTIN

SEPT. 2007
DELHI
ONT

STEAM

TEXT AND PHOTOGRAPHY BY COLIN GARRATT

STEAM

STEAM

AN EVOCATIVE TRIBUTE TO THE LAST DAYS OF STEAM TRAINS

Colin Garratt

Photography and text : Colin Garratt

Publisher: Polly Manguel

Project Editor: Emma Beare

Designer: Peter Maher/Maher Design

Production Manager: Neil Randles

Publishing Assistant: Jo Archer

First published in Great Britain in 2006 by Bounty Books
a division of Octopus Publishing Group Limited
2-4 Heron Quays, London E14 4JP

A CIP catalogue record is available from the British Library

ISBN-13: 978-0-753713-99-0
ISBN-10: 0-753713-99-3

Printed and bound in China

Contents

Introduction

I WRITE THESE WORDS sitting at my desk in Milepost's studios. One field away, clearly visible, is the bridge from which I watched my first trains as a boy of nine. I remember how my young senses were thrilled and overawed by the majestic trains which passed and such a variety, ranging from the elegant, mile a minute "Thames Clyde Express" to the diminutive, four wagon, "smelly bone", chugging its way from Leicester cattle market sidings to the glue factory near Market Harborough. "The bone" was always worked by a superannuated 0-6-0 with an enormously high chimney.

Although only a child, I possessed a distinctive feel for the railway's glorious status; it's great industrial past and it's intrinsic role within the economic structure of society. The whole industrial fabric of our nation had been made possible by the railway; it had changed the face of the world and apart from being Britain's greatest gift to mankind was the safest and most "civilised" form of land transportation. At the heart of this monumentality lay the steam locomotive.

Then, in 1955, the British government announced the modernisation plan under which steam was to be phased out. Concurrent with the dying steam locomotive came Britain's move towards a road based economy; the private motor car made its brash incursion on a popular level, long distance road haulage became prevalent and the emergent motorways heralded the iniquitous Beeching era under which the railway shrank to previously unimaginable proportions.

An entire epoch was drawing to a close, not only in Britain, but across the world too, as country after country declared against steam and, in some cases against railways as well. And so, in 1969, at the age of 29, I made the most important decision of my life; to document, in photographs, the Last Steam Locomotives of the World. The economics and practicalities of the task were daunting; no one had ever made a living photographing trains before. I had no academic qualifications to help me with the task, but I had an instinctive feel for the essential rightness of railways and the vastness of their history; I also had youth on my side and boundless energy and enthusiasm. And in search of a pictorial language, the great painters were studied.

The guiding star of my life's ambition was Turner's painting of "The Fighting Temeriere"; its brilliance of conception and nobility of sentiment provided constant inspiration and before departing on major expeditions, I used to go to the National Gallery and bask in the sheer magic of this picture.

Without exaggeration, I worked at least a hundred hours a week for the first fifteen years of my self imposed odyssey. Each year was divided roughly into three parts; four months on expedition; four months giving nation-wide lectures and audio-visual presentations and four months writing books and carrying out research. It was, from the outset, a desperate race against time.

The enormity of the task inevitably exerted a toll on my personal and family life, despite the fact that in the earlier years I received enormous help from many individuals and valuable sponsorship from such companies as Practica, Canon, Agfa and Electrosonic. I have written some sixty books on railways, travel and photography and covered almost fifty countries embracing all continents but the work will never be finished.

I remember listening to an interview with the folk singer A.L.Lloyd on Radio Four shortly before he died. The young female reporter told him how gratified he must feel having researched and recorded for posterity songs which would otherwise have faded into oblivion. "Not at all" A.L.Lloyd replied solemnly, "my concern is with the ones I haven't found". In the instant, a cold shiver ran up my spine because I know that one day I will be in the same position as A. L. Lloyd and will give the same answer.

It has been reliably estimated that some 640,000 steam locomotives have been built embracing tens of thousands of different types. The steam locomotive is now in its third century as a prime mover following its inception in 1804.

Looking back over the years much valuable work has been done and I hope to retain the physical strength to do much more but I am under no illusion that the steam locomotive, as a commercial force, will outlive me. Now that the steam age is drawing to its close, it is easier to look back with a clear perspective on what is, undeniably, the greatest chapter in man's industrial history. An analogy with natural history and the evolution of species may reasonably be made.

The steam locomotive is a particularly sensual, beautiful and awe inspiring creation. Interest in it will never die and I believe its evolution will be studied avidly by future generations. And that is why I echo the sentiment of A. L. Lloyd, for the pictures I have made represent but a blink amid the infinity of industrial legend

COLIN GARRATT
Milepost 92½
Newton Harcourt
Leicestershire
May 2006

British Industrial, Dockland

AN AFTERNOON VISIT to Preston Dock on Wednesday 20th September 1967 produced this study. Main-line steam was in its final months and the picture was made in between a visit to Lostock Hall Motive Power Depot in the morning and Rose Grove where I ended up in the late afternoon.

The handsome engine illustrated is 'Progress', one of a standard 16-inch design built by Bagnalls of Stafford. The first example appeared in 1934 at Birchenwood coking plant and the final one appeared in 1955.

The class totalled only 18 engines and their distribution was as follows: Nine went to the NCB - Staffs Area where later three were fitted with Giesl ejectors; seven went to the Preston Dock Authority and one each went to the Leicestershire Area Coalfield and to Birchenwood.

It is a sad reflection that 'Progress', Bagnalls and Preston Docks have all faded into history.

Preston's Albert Edward Dock on the River Ribble was once the largest single dock in Europe. It was wonderful to be confronted by this all-embracing scene, complete with fish boxes, chatting workers and period articulated lorries

British Main Line — steam's last great fling

THE MID 1960s were a deeply distressing time; it was evident that the government's modernisation plan of 1955, under which steam traction was to be phased out, would happen and that the steam locomotive, loved by millions, would disappear. As steam was relegated to the more menial tasks, one bright spot remained; the former Southern Railway main line between London Waterloo and Southampton, Bournemouth and Weymouth remained steam worked until July 1967.

The stars of this drama were Bulleid's magnificent Merchant Navy, West Country and Battle of Britain Pacifics ably supported by BR's Standard 5 Class 4-6-0s. Thousands of enthusiasts were attracted from all over Britain. Train crews knew they were handling steam's last great fling and such was the atmosphere that innumerable 100-mph bursts were made, especially over the racing ground between Basingstoke and Woking. Just before the end came, one of the Pacifics was logged at 103 mph with an 11-coach train while another touched 105 mph.

During the last year I covered most of the system and found autumn in the New Forest between Southampton and Bournemouth particularly inspiring. Blackberries abounded in the hedges as the forest turned into an autumn blaze. The Pacific's mournful whistles and the soft pounding intensity of their exhausts was beautiful to experience. As autumn lengthened the forest's mood changed and the flaming sunsets gave way to a misty dampness in which the exhausts of the trains would remain minutes after they had passed. Rainy days added a mystique of their own and although gaps between the trains were sometimes lengthy, one could enjoy nature at its best; wild flowers abounded by the lineside while newts, lizards, snakes, toads and rare butterflies became an everyday sight.

The train of the day was the 'Bournemouth Belle', invariably headed by a Merchant Navy with a spotless rake of Pullman coaches for its 108-mile journey to London, Waterloo.

The final weekend was something we had all dreaded. On the Sunday all steam locomotives surviving in the south west were sent under their own power to Salisbury shed from where they were to be auctioned and dispatched to breakers' yards. I called at Salisbury Depot in the evening and found it crammed full of engines, the majority of which had run down that day. All fires had been dropped yet the engines were still in steam and through the evening silence that hung over the depot could be heard their hissing and gurgling impregnating the air with that acrid aroma so peculiar to steam locomotives. It was as if history were being haunted by its own ghosts. The reminiscences hung heavy on my mind.

Rebuilt Bulleid Pacific No.34021, 'Dartmoor' arrives at Bournemouth Central with an express from Weymouth to London, Waterloo. 'Dartmoor' survived until the end of Southern steam in July 1967 and was broken up by Cashmores at Newport in March 1968. It is an interesting thought that the baby being carried in its mother's arms would now be about 40 years old

ABOVE Shrouded in smoke and steam a British Railway's Standard Class 5MT, 4-6-0 climbs Upwey Bank out of Weymouth with an express for London, Waterloo

British Railways Standard 4MT Class 4-6-0 on an eastbound climb away from Weymouth

Merchant Navy Class No.35008, 'Orient Line', heads an up local through Poole

British Main Line, Shap Bank

SHAP BANK on Britain's West Coast Main Line is one of the world's most celebrated railway photographic locations. The London and North Western Railway used it for publicity shots in the 19th century, the embankment past Shap Wells Hotel being a favourite point. The Bank extends from the village of Tebay to Shap Summit, a distance of some five miles, the steepest sections being 1 in 75. In steam days this constituted a considerable obstacle on a busy line with heavy trains.

The approach from the south was through the awe-inspiring Lune Gorge in which the water troughs at Dillicar were situated. After crossing the River Lune the line swings round through Tebay where many trains would stop for a banker, Tebay shed having an allocation of engines for this purpose.

The famous hotel at Shap Wells is situated about half way up the bank. It opened in 1833, before the railway was built, and invited nobility, gentry and public to savour its conviviality, to use the baths and to drink from the spa well. The hotel prospered throughout the 19th century and the presence of nearby Shap station enabled easy access to visitors who used the hotel as a focal point in the area with commanding views of the railway.

Shap Bank as a railway photographic location received wide publicity after railway photographer Eric Treacy became enraptured with the area. He loved Shap, 'its rolling fells and gurgling becks, its wild loneliness, blue skies, the wild cry of the curlew, the warm welcome of its farms or a cup of tea in the signal box at Scout Green'. But it wasn't just what Eric Treacy wrote about Shap, his pictures totally captured the ambience of the location and the magic of the steam age. His pictures of L.M.S. Princess Royal and Princess Coronation Pacifics toiling up the bank have never been bettered.

It was a great experience to visit Shap even albeit at the very end of the steam age. Staying at Shap Wells was not an option so I stayed at High Scales, the home of Agnes Thackeray and her family, whose farmhouse overlooked the line. It was September 1967, the final months of steam in Britain.

At night I deliberately lay awake and one morning at 01.00 the cry of a 'Britannia's' whistle rang out across the lonely fells as the engine prepared to start the long climb up from Tebay. The barking exhaust, interposed with that of the banker, cut through the stillness as it resounded over the hills as the heavy Pacific fought its way up the gradient with a northbound freight. As I watched its approach from my bedroom window, blazing coals were flung out of the chimney and the cab was bathed in a flickering orange glow that was reflected in the smoke trail. Spellbound, I watched the drama and listened to the rhythms – for surely a living presence was passing through the fells that night.

I remember Agnes telling me that a motorway was to be built through the fells at Shap. I responded with sheer disbelief that so wonderful a place could be defiled.

Today, the hideousness of the M6 has dissipated much of the magic almost as much as the disappearance of steam. The motorway's odious presence is augmented by the fact that it carries much of the Anglo-Scottish traffic that was, and still should be, the preserve of the railway.

My relationship with Shap was renewed 36 years later when in 2003/4 I was commissioned by Virgin Trains to photograph their new tilting Pendolino on 'Test Site A', which was the section of line between Tebay and Carlisle. This time I stayed at Shap Wells Hotel and over several trips made pictures that were widely used by Virgin to advertise their new trains.

Needless to say, while photographing the cutting-edge technology of the 21st century, I realised that a new chapter in the railway history of Shap was just beginning.

British Railways Standard Class 4,
4-6-0 No.75032, approaches
Scout Green signal box while
assisting a northbound freight up
Shap Bank on Wednesday 27th
September 1967

British Main Line — waiting to be towed to the breaker's yard

THE END OF STEAM operation in Britain in August 1968 left many locomotives at depots. Patricroft in Manchester was a typical example; a silent depot, full of dead engines that on sunny days became transformed into mottled effect; Stanier 8Fs, Black 5s and BR Standard 5s being the principal types. The depot had a poignant atmosphere of abandonment and if you had walked down the gangway between the lines of silent engines and gone through the doorway at the far end of the shed, you would have found more engines outside rusting away in weed-covered yards. Some of the 8Fs pictured at Patricroft subsequently were towed to Cohen's Breakers Yard at Kettering. This yard was located on the former Midland Railway ironstone line to Loddington and was in very scenic surroundings.

Traditionally locomotives have been broken up at main railway works. In the final years of steam thousands of locomotives were auctioned to private scrapyards. In the ten years between 1958 and 1968 more than 16,000 steam locomotives were cut up. In March 1959, BR implemented a policy of selling redundant locomotives rather than dispatching them from their own works. In those final years steam engines frequently were seen being towed around the country to dozens of scrapyards, many with names that were destined to become a part of railway history; Cashmore's, Cohen's, Bird's, Woodham Bros., Draper's, R. S. Hayes, King's, Buttigieg's, Central Wagon, Motherwell Machinery and Scrap. In addition there were many little-known yards, often close to where condemned engines were lying, that took very small quantities. In the case of Riddles War Department 2-8-0s that totalled 733 locomotives, many different yards were involved including eight BR works. In the case of Stanier 8Fs, a total of 663 engines were scrapped at 18 different locations the most significant being Cashmore's at Great Bridge who took 219 examples.

A line of ex-LMS Stanier 8F, 2-8-0s
lies condemned at Patricroft depot
following the end of steam work in
Britain in 1968

ABOVE A former LMS Stanier 8F, 2-8-0, stands alongside a British Railways Standard 5, 4-6-0 with Caprotti valve gear at Patricroft following the end of steam working in 1968

LEFT Former LMS Black 5 'Ayrshire Yeomanry', one of only four members of this 842 strong class to be named. Patricroft 1968

France

DURING WORLD WAR TWO, the French National Railway suffered widespread damage and at the time of the liberation only 3,000 of their 17,000 pre-war locomotives were in a serviceable condition. Such a state of affairs was the result of sabotage during the German occupation, Allied bombardments and destruction brought about by the retreating enemy. Further to this, many locomotives had been taken away by the Germans for use in other countries.

A state of emergency existed and France appealed to America for help. In December 1944, a group from the French Railway Mission went to the Baldwin Locomotive Works in Philadelphia to discuss a new design of a 2-8-2 mixed-traffic engine capable of hauling 800-tonne trains on level tracks at 65mph.

On the 3rd November 1945 the first four arrived in France, the initial engine carrying the name 'Liberation', so giving an appropriate name for the whole class. Between 1945 and 1947 1,340 engines were supplied, although only 1,323 arrived, 17 being lost at sea en route. Classified 141R, the type came from Baldwin, Alco, Lima and The Canadian Locomotive Company of Montreal.

Superb engines in all respects, the 141Rs were destined to dominate the steam scene in France until the end. Another American standard design also existed in the SNCF's ranks in the form of the United States Army Transportation Corps 0-6-0Ts that were surplus to requirements after the war.

These war-associated designs were contrasted by two celebrated and varied types of pure French extraction; the 140C Class 2-8-0s and the lovely 231G Pacifics. The 140Cs numbered 370 engines and were of an Etat design of 1913. They played an important role during World War One and were the French equivalent of the Railway Operating Division 2-8-0s in Britain originally designed by Robinson for the Great Central Railway. The last 140Cs were allocated appropriately to Verdun, the scene of much bitter fighting in both world wars.

In contrast, the 231G Pacifics ended a long tradition of elegant four-cylinder compound thoroughbreds in the purest of French traditions. Known as 'Les Belles Machines', one of their last duties was working the 'Golden Arrow' from Calais to Paris until 1969 when they were replaced by diesels.

The 231Gs were the epitome of beauty and power although in celebration of the latter-day, all-purpose, mixed-traffic Mikado, it must be recorded that in March 1970, a 141R deputised for a failed diesel and worked the 'Golden Arrow' express from Calais to Amiens and kept time perfectly.

Sunlight, smoke and shadow surround two former Est Railway 141TB Class tanks in the round house at Nogent Vincennes Depot in Paris

ABOVE One of the SNCF's classic 141R 2-8-2s heads out of Narbonne with a mixed freight

TOP LEFT An SNCF 141R Class 2-8-2 crosses the viaduct at Rivesaltes heading northwards with a perishables train from the Spanish border

LEFT The southbound Fléche d'Or ('Golden Arrow') headed by a former PLM 231G Class Pacific threads through a lineside apple orchard south of Rang-du-Fliers on Saturday 13th April 1968

Iron Mountain, Austria

THE IRON MOUNTAIN RAILWAY was one of the most interesting and exciting steam-worked lines in Europe. It was located at the eastern end of the Austrian Alps and its purpose was to convey iron ore from the Erzberg, a 2,400ft mountain of solid iron ore, to the steel works at Donawitz. The line began at Vordenberg and the 12½ mile section to Eisenerz had a ruling gradient of 1 in 14 necessitating the use of the Abt System of rack operation over many stretches. At Vordenberg, a connection with Austrian Railways' electrified line was made for the short journey onwards to Donawitz.

The Iron Mountain Railway opened in 1891 and soon came under the auspices of the Austrian State Railway. The original engines were supplied in 1890 by Floridsdorf of Vienna in the form of four-cylinder, rack-and-adhesion 0-6-2Ts that remained at work into the 1970s.

In 1912 Karl Golsdorf, the Chief Mechanical Engineer of the Austrian State Railways, designed some 0-12-0Ts to increase the lines' capacity; considerable side play was given in the first, fifth and sixth axle.

World War Two produced a huge increase in the demand for iron ore and after the annexation of Austria the German State Railway produced two giant 2-12-2Ts in 1941. These also were built by Floridsdorf and could haul 400-tonne trains over 1-in-14 grades at nine miles an hour. A passenger service was also operated, including a shuttle between Vordenberg and Vordenberg Markt, the journey over the line was a real experience.

To stand on the mountainside between Vordenberg and Prabichl watching a procession of empty trains storming up the 1 in 14 with a locomotive at either end, was a rare experience; the engines' pounding rhythms echoing and reverberating across the mountains providing a poignant contrast to the Alpine stillness.

Smoke, steam and speed on
Austria's Iron Mountain Railway
as a 97 Class 0-6-2T blasts away
from Erzberg with a loaded iron-
ore train on 1st July 1970

An Austrian Railways' Class 97
Class 0-6-2T makes a laboured
ascent over the Iron Mountain
Railway between Erzberg and
Prabichl with a loaded ironstone
train

This scene in the yard at Lopez Industrias Zaragoza, shows ex-Spanish Rio Tinto Railway No.15 that was built by Beyer Peacock of Manchester as their No. 3345 in 1875

Spanish Industrial

SCRAP TANKS were one of the rarest forms of locomotive, they were built from the remains of older engines that had been broken up. Scotland's Highland Railway had some and I found one in northern Spain in April 1971.

Named 'Bilbao', she was a beautifully proportioned 5ft 6in-gauge 2-4-0T with high-stepping wheels and worked on the Turon complex that formed part of the Hunosa colliery group in northern Spain.

'Bilbao' was put together in 1921 at Turon works but the origin of the parts is unknown. She shunted the colliery yard at Turon that included metre and 660mm gauge tracks for various routes to the complex of mines.

Many of Spain's industrial veterans achieved centenarian status. The best example is at the Tharsis Sulphur and Copper Company in the south that has a derelict Dubs 0-4-0ST dating back to 1867 while marooned on a ledge, halfway down a vast pit, is a Dubs 0-6-0T of 1881. The amazing Hartmann 0-8-0 at Olloniego is covered separately in this book. Engines from many European countries found their way to Spanish industrial environments and it would be difficult to imagine anywhere where the locomotives were more varied in terms of their design, age, origin and character.

BELOW 'Bilbao', a 5ft 6in-gauge Turon-built 2-4-0 scrap tank shunts the yard at Turon while a 600mm-gauge 0-4-0T lies derelict

ABOVE Silent sentinels at the abandoned Rio Tinto Railway in southern Spain; 10th May 1987

ABOVE The Tharsis Sulphur and Copper Company, Spain, operated this Dubs 0-4-0T named 'Saucita' of 1867. She is seen here abandoned in the old working on 7th May 1987

West Germany

THE SHOCK OF MAIN-LINE steam traction ending in Britain in August 1968 made nearby countries such as West Germany appear very attractive. Although heavily modernised, steam still survived there – and in the form of some very potent types.

In the summer of 1969, just a few weeks before I turned professional, I made a two-week camping expedition to Germany to visit some of the principal steam routes. These were Rheine to Emden in the north, with Class 50, 2-10-0s, O12 Class Pacifics and O42 Class 2-8-2s; the Moselle Valley route from Koblenz to Trier with its superb O44 Class, three-cylinder 2-10-0s and O23 Class 2-6-2s and the Paderborn to Altenbeken line with Class 50 2-10-0s.

In the early 1920s, German State Railways implemented a locomotive standardisation plan and some of the last surviving types were derived from this, including the O44 Class of 1926, almost two thousand of which were in service by 1945. The two-cylinder Class 50, 2-10-0 was a lightweight version that first appeared from

Henschel in 1939. Over three thousand were in service by 1943, some having been built in countries occupied by Germany during World War Two. These engines formed the basis for Germany's Kreigslokomotiv or War Engine, an austerity version of the 50s that totalled over six thousand examples, making them one of the most numerous steam types in history. The Kreigsloks spread to almost every European country, either as a result of Germany's war action or in reparation packages given to aggrieved countries following the war.

Main-line steam building continued in Germany until 1959 when the last of just over a hundred Class O23 Prairies was put into traffic. Interestingly this was within a year of steam-building finally ceasing in Britain.

However, the most flamboyant West German locomotives were the three-cylinder O12 Pacifics of 1939. These were true Pacific racehorses complete with 6ft 7in-diameter driving wheels and were worthy successors to the Bullied Pacifics we had enjoyed in Britain just three summers earlier.

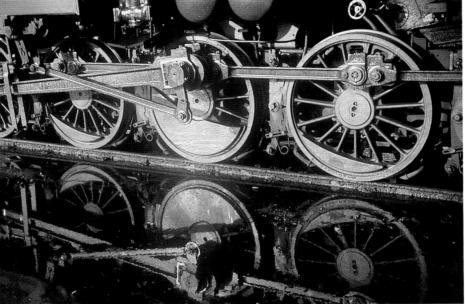

FAR LEFT Sunrise in the Mosel Valley as a German 44 Class, three-cylinder 2-10-0 heads an early freight bound for Trier

LEFT The driving wheels of a German Class 44, three-cylinder 2-10-0

LEFT A brace of German Class 44, three-cylinder 2-10-0s cross the river at Bullay in the Mosel Valley against a hillside covered with vineyards in this famous wine-producing region. The engines are in charge of a three-thousand tonne coal train heading for Trier

Italy

THE ITALIAN SCHOOL of locomotive design was highly distinctive and dated back to 1905 when Guiseppi Zara produced twelve standard designs for the newly formed Italian State Railway. It was to be almost 50 years before the same thing happened in Britain. By 1930 steam locomotive construction in Italy had almost ceased.

Most of my work in Italy was carried out during April and May of 1976 as part of a six-month expedition by motor caravan covering Austria, Greece, Turkey, and Syria.

Sadly, the number of pictures I managed to get in Italy were limited, partly because of the sparsity of traffic on the secondary lines of the north and partly because of the flat, featureless landscape that I always thought of as a cabbage patch.

It was frustrating because the period look of the engines was so appealing with their spring-balance safety valves, stove-pipe chimneys, conical smoke-box doors, round-top fireboxes and non-side window cabs.

My priority in Italy was to document the Franco-Crosti-boilered 743 Class that was a modification of the standard 740 Class 2-8-0s of 1911.

The Franco-Crosti boiler was an Italian innovation that maximized the use of hot gases from the firebox. Having traversed the boiler in the normal way, the gases were fed back through two large pre-heater drums containing the boiler-feed water. The gases were then exhausted from a chimney on either side of the engine at the firebox end and were at a much lower temperature than on conventional engines. A fuel saving of ten per cent was achieved.

In 1955 some 740s were rebuilt with a single pre-heater slung underneath the main boiler and reclassified 741. In principle this was the same as earlier rebuilds except that the pre-heater drum was largely concealed

and only one chimney was necessary; predictably this was placed on the fireman's side. It is said that these modifications led to Britain imposing sanctions on Italy in 1936 because until that time Italy had been dependent on British coal. It is an interesting twist of fate that some of Britain's standard 9F Class 2-10-0s of 1954 were built with Crosti boilers.

I worked long and hard over the secondary lines of northern Italy chasing avidly between Pavia and Cremona for 743s. Some good work was done around the rape fields near Roggione. In contrast, I did cover the 741s on the scenic route through the Dolomite mountains from Fortezza on the Italian/Austrian border to San Candido.

Later I met the Italian author Claudio Pedronitzi who said he knew a reliable laboratory that could process the Franco-Crosti films. Foolishly I let them go and they came back badly impaired through faulty processing.

It was a heart-breaking situation after weeks of intense effort made even worse by the fact that I hadn't time to repeat the effort and that more than half of the surviving Franco-Crostis had been withdrawn by that time.

Fortunately, this was the only time during 30 years of world expeditions that I experienced faulty processing.

Italian Railways' Franco-Crosti Class 743, 2-8-0 No.301 heads a Pavia to Cremona pick-up goods away from Corteolone on Saturday 29th April 1976

ABOVE As evening shadows lengthen an Italian Railways 625 Class 2-6-0 leaves Noale-Scorze with a Venice to Bassano train.

TOP RIGHT Italian 743 Class Franco Crosti No.301 near Roggione with the 08.45 Cremona to Pavia goods. Thursday 22nd April 1976

BOTTOM RIGHT Italian Railways 741 Crosti boilered 2-8-0 on the San Candido to Fortezza line in the dolomite mountains. April 1971

BOTTOM LEFT An Italian Railways 880 Class 2-6-0T at Novara on Tuesday 24th August 1971

Adventures at Pennyvenie Mine, Scotland

IN MAY 1972 I embarked on a tour of Scottish coalfields the highlight of which was my visit to the Waterside system at Dalmellington in Ayrshire. One of the last havens of industrial steam in Scotland, it was located in the upper valley of the River Doon, an area rich in coal and ironstone that gave rise to the Dalmellington Iron Company in 1845. This was to become a major industrial complex, the company's lines spreading out far into the surrounding hills.

The story was eloquently told by David Smith in his classic book 'The Dalmellington Iron Company' that reads like a full-bloodied adventure story. Its pages abound with industrial legend. After the ironworks closed, the colliery system continued with coal being taken away by British Rail from the exchange sidings at Waterside where the ironworks was situated.

With tales of the old iron company on my mind, I walked from Dalmellington village along the lonely road to Waterside. It was a perfect morning. Although the sun had barely risen, it was already flooding the valley with light and the glistening foliage, soaked with a heavy summer dew, echoed the sun's brilliance causing a thousand twinkling flashes at each step I took.

As I approached Waterside, No.21, a standard 16-inch Andrew Barclay 0-4-0ST was busily preparing to take a rake of empties up to Pennyvenie Colliery. Appropriately,

all Dalmellington's locomotives came from nearby Andrew Barclay's works in Kilmarnock.

The traditional mainstay was the 16-inch, 0-4-0ST but in 1913 Dalmellington took delivery of an 18-inch, 0-6-0T that was numbered 17. She was known as the 'Big Yin' and had been on the system for some 60 years. I was told how the Big Yin once took 43 empty wagons and ten loaded ones – altogether upwards of 500 tonnes – up a sinuous 1-in-66 bank, notwithstanding the tremendous amount of friction at the buffers and flanges due to the uneven track.

Over a 40-year period 18 of these engines were built by Andrew Barclay for use in collieries and ironworks and three worked on the Dalmellington complex.

The enginemen on the system were extremely friendly and I rode footplate from Waterside to Minnivey and Pennyvenie on No.21, a 16-inch engine of 1949. Along with all the other engines she had a cut-down, wooden-bodied wagon attached to act as an auxiliary tender.

The rakes were long and the track steeply graded necessitating some blow ups. These enabled me to do some lineside photography in the glorious scenery. The colliery yard at Pennyvenie was especially photogenic; the cry of curlews floated down from the surrounding hills while the beautiful song of a woodlark erupted from a lineside fence.

Andrew Barclay 0-4-0ST+T No.21 of 1949 complete with crew and improvised tender made from a cut-down coal wagon, on the Waterside system at Dalmellington in May 1972. When working hard on the run up to Pennyvenie Colliery, these engines could consume two tonnes of coal per shift. The improvised tenders enabled the engines to work for several days without coaling

TOP LEFT AND BOTTOM RIGHT
Dalmellington No.21, an Andrew
Barclay 0-4-0ST+T of 1949
prepares to leave Pennyvenie
Mine with a loaded train for the
BR exchange on 15th May 1972

TOP RIGHT Dalmellington 0-6-0T
No.17, Andrew Barclay 1913,
trips up to the shale bank on 15th
May 1972

Ladies of Blaenavon, Wales

WHEN THE SOUTH-WALES coalfield was being developed between 1750 and 1800, huge deposits of coal, iron and limestone were found in the hills around Blaenavon at the head of the Eastern Valley. By 1789 the first iron foundry was put into operation and the night skies glowed crimson. Blaenavon iron was destined to girdle the earth.

When I visited Blaenavon in early 1973 it was an industrial ghost town; the last two steam locomotives worked a pathetically small opencast mine amid otherwise barren hillsides. The brooding atmosphere of a revolution spent hung heavy. The misery, exploitation and full-blooded drama of industrial Blaenavon was eloquently told in Alec Cordell's novel 'Rape of the Fair Country'.

The old locoshed stood exposed in the middle of the wasteland. The wind howled mournfully through the structures and every few minutes the roof gave a sickening lurch. This place belonged to another age. As I left snowflakes carried on the wind and 'Nora', one of Blaenavon's Andrew Barclay 0-4-0STs, passed on its way to the shed. The wind blew as cold as charity and so grey was the afternoon that twilight had begun by 15.00. I struggled down the hillside towards town, passing an abandoned steam crane, its derelict form looking like the skeleton of a dinosaur. I reached Broad Street half frozen and arrived at The Lion where a roaring coal fire in the snug quickly restored me.

Next morning at The Lion I met J. T. Morgan, a sprightly 90 year old and what a tale he could tell: 'We were the workshop of the world when I was a boy'. He described the fiery skies and the coal being sent to Cardiff docks for locomotives and steam ships throughout the British Empire. He recalled the huge trainloads of iron and steel leaving Blaenavon bound for Pontypool. He took pride in telling me how the tyres for the Great Western 'King Class' were made on Forgeside. And the Ladies of Blaenavon? Yes, he remembered all of them; 'Betty', 'Chrissie', 'Gina', 'Jean', 'Joan', 'Lily', 'Nan', 'Nora' and another engine named 'Toto'; all saddle tanks and all from Andrew Barclay of Kilmarnock. Because, he explained, Mr. Clements, the manager of the old Blaenavon Iron Company, and his engineer were Scottish. He could not tell me who the girls were but promised to find out.

J. T. Morgan subsequently spoke to Miss Lily Jones, once secretary to Mr. Clements, who claimed that one engine was named after her and Nora was the daughter of another manager from the Blaenavon Iron Company. She also suggested that engines were named after Mr. Clements' four daughters and that 'Toto' had been their family dog.

In the accompanying picture 'Nora' and 'Toto' are depicted colouring Blaenavon's skies with fire and so evoke memories of those halcyon days two centuries gone when the skies glowed crimson from the world's first iron foundries.

Former Blaenavon Iron Company
Andrew Barclay 0-4-0STs eke out
their final days. Left is 'Toto' and right
is 'Nora', built at Andrew Barclay's
Caledonia works in Kilmarnock in
1917 and 1920 respectively

Hafod rhy nys

THE FOLLOWING TWO PICTURES, made over a year apart, are improvisations on a theme. I have always enjoyed returning to specific locations, sometimes years later, to re-interpret a drama under different conditions and to reflect the passing of time. The first picture was made on Monday 20th December 1971 on a tour of the South Wales coalfield. The derelict structures of man's industrial past dominate the foreground as the colliery's No.4, a Hunslet Austerity 0-6-0ST, clanks a string of grimy wagons back to the pit head. The world's first steam locomotive was born in the adjacent valley in 1804. Clearly this is the end of an epoch; the semi-derelict, slag-ridden valleys bear witness to a revolution spent.

A further visit to the South Wales coalfield in 1973 enabled this variation to be made. The picture is dated Monday 26th February 1973. A fall of snow has transformed the greyness of the valley floor into a shimmering white texture. But the depression inevitably remains; steam oozes from the ailing locomotive; more glass has fallen out of the windows with the passing of time; the water washes timelessly down the valley sides and the skies of South Wales seem perennially grey.

One of the most stimulating aspects of photography is to return to specific locations to make variations on a theme. It is possible to develop an empathy with certain places that becomes part of one's thinking and psyche. This way of interpreting the pictorial dramas of our time was not restricted to photography but applied equally to painters too

Wreck of Tithorea, Greece

ON SATURDAY 14TH APRIL 1973 I began a working relationship with 'The Wreck of Tithorea', an Austrian Empire-inspired 2-10-0 that lay abandoned at Tithorea on the main line between Athens and Thessaloniki.

The engine was based on Karl Golsdorf's 580 Class for the Austrian State Railways. He was their CME from 1891 to 1916 and produced about 50 designs that, as a family of engines, were as exciting aesthetically as any produced in the history of railways.

The wreck's front had been badly damaged and the engine taken out of traffic, pushed to the southern end of the old depot yard and forgotten. Numbered 908 by Greek Railways, she was built by Staatseisenbahn Gesellschaft of Vienna in 1926 and was one of 40 such engines once operated by Greek Railways. I never managed to ascertain any details of the crash or where and when and why it happened. The wreck was very atmospheric and I was intensely attracted to it. On that first visit the pictures were made in spring sunlight amid a carpet of wild flowers.

Six and a half years later, in October 1979, I returned to Tithorea as part of a Greek graveyard expedition – all steam working having finished by that time. Did the wreck still exist? Not only was it still present but the rust had deepened to an exotic dark red and a small bush had begun to grow in the smokebox. The golden October sunlight provided a perfect foil for photography.

I also did some photography of the wreck in the dark. It was an eerie experience visiting that lonely coppice at night, the engine exuded a strange presence and I was reminded of the Insular Lumber Company's Mallet No.7 that was widely known on the Philippine island of Negros as a weird engine. But the days were warm and pleasant and there was much to photograph as the wreck had been joined by many recently withdrawn S160 2-8-0s and Baldwin 2-10-0s dating back to World War Two. The depot had long been abandoned but around the old offices many grapevines remained. These were laden with huge purple grapes that provided ready and delightful sustenance throughout the days.

The 'Wreck of Tithorea' had become a distinct part of my photographic work and the Greek graveyard expedition of August and September 1982 enabled me to return to Tithorea for a third time. This time I spent a week there, not just with the wreck but once again covering the many other engines dumped there. On this visit I embarked on two further night themes of the wreck. One of these was based on a colony of bats that lived in the surrounding coppice. At dusk they could be seen flying around the engine and I endeavoured to include them in a picture but with no success.

More successful were the lamp-and-thistle themes; these consisted of a rusty lamp in the foreground along with some dead thistles. The lamp echoed the front of the locomotive while the dead thistles of high summer echoed its rusty tones.

At the end of that week I bade farewell to the wreck. I was never to see it again but it had been an engaging part of my life over a period of some ten years.

The bats and owls that frequent the lonely coppice in which the 'Wreck of Tithorea' lay served to highlight the organic atmosphere of that place. I have tried to show something of the brooding presence that emanated from this haunted locomotive in these photographs

STEAM

A theme made near Stanjel in August 1972 of a Yugoslav State Railway 33 Class 2-10-0. These were actually German Kreigsloks, many of which remained in use in Yugoslavia following World War Two and worked turn about with Prussian G12 2-10-0s and former Austrian Empire types in Slovenia

Yugoslavia

MY FIRST EXPEDITION TO Yugoslavia was in July/August 1972. I was fortunate to meet and travel with the Yugoslav railway historian and author Tadej Brate. Tadej lived in Ljubljana, the capital of Slovenia, and knew the republic's steam lines intimately. His authoritative book 'Steam Locomotives of Yugoslavia' is the definitive work on the subject. Political and territorial upheavals as a result of two world wars bequeathed to Yugoslavia an incredible richness of locomotive designs, types and backgrounds.

It was unfortunate that most of Yugoslavia was hostile to railway photography, particularly Serbia and Bosnia where, quite apart from the main lines, many rare types of engine were active in industrial environments.

I learned from Tadej the sheer beauty of Golsdorf's locomotives of the old Austrian State Railway because direct derivatives of some of Golsdorf's principal creations were active in Slovenia, including 2-8-0s, 0-10-0s and 2-10-0s. We had great adventures together including a two-day trip on the rickety single-track line from Ljubljana to Kocevje with the 25 Class 2-8-0s. These engines were direct descendants of Golsdorf's 170 Class, two-cylinder compounds of 1897 of which some nine hundred were built. The Kocevje line passed through tiny villages where time appeared to stand still. Having intercepted a Class 25 on line, we chased it avidly by car. Tadej knew the area well and we bounced crazily over un-made roads in our attempts to get ahead of the train. I will never forget the sheer magic of photographing that Golsdorf engine. It had an aura of mystique and introduced me to a new school of locomotive design.

No less exciting were our adventures on the Jesenice to Nova Gorica line with the 28 Class 0-10-0s that were a derivative of Golsdorf's original 180 Class. I loved the way the engines smokily fought their way up the bank from Prvacina to the summit at Stanjel where we spent many happy days. I will never forget the long chases we made with the 28s as they climbed through the valley. In the sweltering heat we pursued them for mile after mile and arrived in Stanjel soaked in sweat where we assuaged ourselves with the cool joys of a station water pump. Also

on this line were some ex-Prussian G12, three-cylinder 2-10-0s, classified Yugoslav State Railway 36 Class. I can place on record that Tadej is the only person I have ever encountered who could run faster than I could when chasing locomotives.

My next expedition to Yugoslavia was 11 years later when my target was the Yugoslav State Railways' 51 Class 2-6-2Ts, former Hungarian Railway 375 Class. I had tried to cover these locomotives on the 1972 expedition when, after days battling with the authorities in Belgrade, I achieved restricted permission to photograph a Class 51 at Novi Sad depot.

However, halfway through the session a police van arrived with a large blue light flashing on top, five uniformed officers leapt out in pure Keystone Cops fashion and surrounded my tripod and camera. The 51s were working passenger and mixed trains along the lightly laid line between Karlovac and Sisak, a distance of 63 miles. They had been retained on account of their light axle loading and apparently had worked the line ever since it was built in 1907.

From Karlovac I travelled south to Belgrade to talk to the Ministry of Transport about photographing the elegant Serbian 01 Class Prairies that once worked express trains between Belgrade, Zagreb and Nis, including the twice weekly Orient Express. The officials were reluctant to give me permission to go out in search of 01s. As fast as they claimed that one shed didn't have them, I came up with another that did. Then they decided that none was working so I asked if I could go to see one that was dead. No, they didn't think there was much point in that.

After tremendous pressure from the British Embassy the authorities relented and said that they would produce an 01; it would be in steam and clean and I would be able to photograph it but I would have to pay and wait a month. Waiting a month was secondary to the price – £1,500 – that was impossible!

Bitterly disappointed I began negotiations for another priority; the Serbian Class 20 Moguls that worked the Sid to Bijeljina line but this was also refused. Undeterred, I was determined to go to Sid and negotiate the necessary permission locally. There I was fortunate to meet Sasa Milanovic who spoke excellent English and worked for the regional radio station.

He suggested an interview and next day I was on air, with an interpreter, telling of the historical importance of the Class 20s and how they were part of Germany's master plan to dominate all territories from Berlin to Baghdad following collusion with the Ottoman Empire. The plan was thwarted by the outbreak of the Balkan War and the Class 20s were seized by the Serbian army for their own military purposes.

The interview proved to be the catalyst for receiving authority to photograph on the line to Bijeljina and also in Sid's locomotive shed where five Class 20s were allocated. The type had been designed by Borsig of Berlin during that builder's preoccupation with English aesthetics and the 20s definitely had a distinct north-Staffordshire appearance.

RIGHT The 19.10 train from Maribor to Bleiburg on the Austrian border prepares to leave Ruse behind one of the Yugoslav State Railway's handsome 18 Class 4-6-2Ts in August 1972

FAR RIGHT Yugoslav State Railways' 51 Class 2-6-2T at the fire-raking and water stop at Vrginmost on the Karlovac to Sisak line in August 1983

BOTTOM RIGHT A brace of Yugoslav State Railway's 51 Class seen at sunset in Karlovac on 16th August 1983. In front is No.51.144 and to the rear No.51.024

Portugal

PORTUGAL'S BEAUTIFUL Douro Valley had some of Europe's finest steam railways. The main line through the valley ran from Oporto in the east to Barca d'Alva on the Spanish border in the west, a distance of 125 miles. Soon after leaving Oporto the line joins the river at Pala and follows it for the remainder of the journey. A wonderful variety of 5ft 6in-gauge steam locomotives could be seen including graceful inside-cylinder 4-6-0s of 1910 and an outside-cylinder version dating back to 1913, both types from Henschel of Kassel.

There was also de Glehn compound 4-6-0s, 2-6-4 and 2-8-4Ts and a solitary four-cylinder compound 2-8-0 built by Schwartzkopf of Berlin to an original North British design of 1912. This engine often worked the heavy overnight mixed from Oporto to Regua.

In addition to these delights, four meter-gauge feeder lines joined the Douro Valley route: the Tamega Line, Arco de Baulhe to Livracao; the Corgo Line, Chaves to Regua; the Tua Line, Braganca to Tua and the Sabor Line, Duas Ingrejas to Pochino. These meter-gauge connections brought a delightful variety of motive power ranging from two 2-4-6-0 compound Mallets to Emil Kessler 0-6-0Ts of 1889.

At the time of my visit in April 1971 no diesels were permitted east of Regua on account of axle loading, an exception being a daily railcar from Salamanca.

I loved the Douro Valley for its tranquillity and freedom from roads, its engines, the friendliness and warmth of the locomotive crews, a swig of wine on the footplate or the invitation to a glass of port in a lineside village. Here, in the heart of the port-producing country, folk are proud to hand a glass or two of their produce to a traveller.

In absolute contrast to the Douro Valley were the busy meter-gauge services that radiated out of Oporto Trindade station. Apart from serving the suburbs, the lines ran far out to the north and south of the city. The complex comprised a circular system 94 miles round and embraced Trindade with Senhora da Hora, Povoa, Famalicao, Lousado, Guimares, Fafe and Trofa. The Trindade to Senhora section was a double-track, meter-gauge main line and during rush hours saw dense traffic. The system was one hundred per cent steam worked with a glorious variety of vintage locomotives such as Emil Kessler 2-6-0Ts of 1886 that had a charming Emmett-like appearance and four-cylinder compound 0-4-4-0 Mallets of 1905.

Rush hour at Trindade was the closest one could get to a Victorian suburban railway. The quaint engines with their gleaming brasswork and copper-capped chimneys looked strange against the modern office blocks that towered high above the station.

Here the city's commuter fraternity comes on weekday mornings; a Mallet rumbles out of the tunnel pulling a rattling string of ancient four-wheel coaches and with billowing brown smoke issuing from its chimney, the engine hisses to a stop amid an aura of luxurious Victoriana. The last thing one expects to see emerging from such a train is a crowd of smartly suited businessmen and office girls. This is Trindade, a haven of antiquity in a restless modern city. The trams rumble overhead, wraiths of steam ooze from the tunnel mouth and the delicate aroma of coffee from a nearby factory permeates the air.

The atmosphere is perhaps best summed up by a train journey I took from Trindade to Senhora on a hot day

BELOW My twin sons Antaeus and Dominion explore abandoned Portuguese locomotives in the graveyard at Vila Nova de Gia on Wed 9th May, 2001. The engine on the left is 2-8-4T No 0184 and on the right 2-8-0 No 701.

with the coach windows wide open. With a shriek from the Mallet's whistle we started with a jerk and as the rattling, four-wheeled coaches entered the tunnel, smoke billowed in through the swirling blackness, window blinds flapped wildly and the shadowy form of other passengers could just be discerned through the dull orange glow of the carriage lamps.

At the front, the Mallet coughed its way through the tunnel with a whiss and the spitting of steam that created polyphony with the exhaust beats.

Victoriana lived again, sending one's imagination back in time to wander through the images of a past era until, after bursting out into the sunshine, the rocking little coach with its hard, wooden seats slowly cleared of smoke. A glance at the passengers showed them to be completely accustomed to all this and a glance through the window revealed new blocks of concrete flats and one was reminded that this was the 20th century after all.

Exactly 30 years later, in April 2001, I returned to Portugal. The country had modernised out of all recognition, not least in its development of roads and its

excess of traffic. The Douro Valley line now terminated at Pochino and no longer connected with Spain. of course it was diesel operated although several rusting 2-4-6-0 Mallets still lay at Regua.

Suburban services from Trindade were also no longer steam but south of the city, at Vile Nova de Gain, I found a line of abandoned 5ft 6in-gauge locomotives in an advanced state of decay having been there for at least 30 years. Included was No.282, one of the inside-cylinder 4-6-0s. Very few such engines existed. They were of a period before World War One and only one engine is preserved in Britain. It occurred to me that this Portuguese example was the only other one in existence.

No.282 had a period, Edwardian aura and looked like a London and North Western 'Prince of Wales' or 'Experiment' – Henschel almost certainly having been influenced by the London and North Western's extensive use of this type of engine.

However, in view of the advanced state of decay, preservation is not an option 2nd the survival of these engines is something of a mystery.

ABOVE Portuguese Railways' meter-gauge 2-4-6-0 Mallet lies abandoned in the old depot at Regua in April 2001

RIGHT Portuguese Railways' inside-cylinder 4-6-0 No.282 lies abandoned at Vile Nova de Gaia in May 2001

ABOVE A Portuguese Railways'
0-4-4-0, four-cylinder Mallet at
Oporto Trindade station making a
wonderful contrast with the
towering apartment blocks of this
stylish city

LEFT A night train from Sernada to
Aviero leaves behind a Portuguese
Railways meter-gauge Orenstein
and Koppel 2-6-0T

Taiwan

IN 1895 CHINA'S DEFEAT in the Sino-Japanese war, led to the island of Taiwan being annexed by Japan. This led to a railway infrastructure that mirrored Japan's with a principal gauge of 3ft 6in and a secondary one of 2ft 6in compared with the predominant standard gauge of the Chinese mainland.

In 1945, following World War Two, the island, previously known as Formosa, returned to China – but only briefly. In 1949 it was declared independent when the Nationalist forces, led by Chiang Kai Shek, fled there in the face of the Communist uprising under Mao Zedong.

There were two separate phases of Japanese steam locomotive design; the European period up to 1919 and the subsequent Japanese period up to the end of steam. Taiwan received the principal Japanese designs, three of which are included in the accompanying picture: On the left is the heavy Consolidation of the European phase, Class DT850 that was Japanese National Railways' 9600 Class first introduced in 1919 as main-line freight engines; in the middle is a mixed-traffic Mogul, Class RCT150 also of the European phase that was Japanese National Railways' Class 8620 introduced in 1914. On the right is a Class DT650 Mikado, a Japanese National Railways' Class D51; 1,100 of these were built between 1936 and 1945. These engines epitomised the Japanese style. This line up was made at Hsinchu on the island's west-coast main line on Wednesday 2nd October 1974.

Unfortunately, the scene doesn't show a Pacific. Japan became famous for Pacifics and had some of the most sensuously beautiful examples ever built with long, low-slung boilers; fireboxes behind the coupled wheels; enormous windshields; large Boxpok driving wheels and tall stovepipe chimneys. Japanese Pacifics also have a delightful slender-waisted appearance. Hsinchu proved to be a wonderful centre with Pacifics on passenger duties, D51 Mikados on freight, Moguls on station pilot duties and three dusty looking DT850s – known as 'Old Oxens' – on yard shunt and local goods work. These delights ensured that Hsinchu was a town well laced with smoke and chime whistles.

Three Taiwan Government Railway classes boil up outside the depot at Hsinchu on Taiwan's west coast main line. Left to right are Classes DT580, 2-8-0; RCT150, 2-6-0 and DT650, 2-8-2 Mikado. These corresponded with the Japanese National Railway Classes 9600, 8620 and D51 respectively

Witbank Shed, South Africa

AT THE TIME OF MY VISIT in 1973, the Witbank area of the South African Transvaal was one of the richest steam-hunting grounds in the world. On the main-line 3ft 6in-gauge to Pretoria and Johannesburg, traffic was heavy, not least because of the number of collieries in the Witbank area.

The huge steam depot at Witbank was full of atmosphere with shafts of strong sunlight penetrating the swirling steam and dense smoke inside. Here I was able to make a set of pictures that were improvisations on a theme.

Apart from the pictorial dramas, the scenes had an important rhetorical aspect as they highlighted the distinction between the last of the pure British school of locomotive design and exports to South Africa. This was represented by the 15AR Class 4-8-2 built by Beyer Peacock of Manchester in 1920 and the first American-designed engines introduced in 1925 in the form of the 15CA/Bs.

South African Railways had decided to try some American locomotives and the success of the 15CA/Bs led them to exert a fundamental influence on South African steam-locomotive design for the remainder of its existence.

American influences accordingly were destined to appear in the 15F, 23, 25; 16D/E Pacifics and 19D Classes.

It was particularly interesting to compare their robust trans-Atlantic features with the pure British homespun products that had been downgraded from the main line into colliery service and were to be found in large numbers on the Witbank area coalfield.

The Witbank coalfield on South Africa's Transvaal was a superb place for finding obsolete main line engines, Here a Class 1 4-8-0, introduced for the Natal Government Railway in 1924, draws a massive rake of wagons at the New Clydesdale Colliery on Thursday 24th May 1973

South African Railways' American inspired 'Big Bill' 4-8-2s Class 15CA/B with (above) a pure British Class 15AR, 4-8-2 in the depot at Witbank on South Africa's Transvaal. Maybe you can smell the oil and so glean something of the incredible atmosphere of these last cathedrals of steam

Coalfields and Goldfields, South Africa

THERE WERE SOME ENORMOUS colliery networks in South Africa with a fine range of different types of locomotive. The majority were ageing period pieces dispensed from main-line service but others were purely industrial designs. In general, the colliery engines of the republic were of main-line proportions, especially in the later years.

This draws a marked distinction between the colliery systems in Europe and other parts of the world but in South Africa feeders to the main-line network are not only lengthy – 20 miles is not unusual – but steeply graded with tracks undulating like corrugated iron. Landau and Wolverkrans Colliery near Witbank were excellent with a mixture of main-line and pure industrial types.

My great favourite on these collieries were the 12A Class 4-8-2s, a type that dated back to 1919. Landau had them painted red and Wolverkrans blue. Landau also had a former Rhodesia Railways 16th Class Garratt that dated back to 1929. She had a superb 1920s lineage and was not dissimilar to the L.M.S. Garratts that Beyer Peacock were building at that time.

Another favourite was the North British 4-8-2T industrial. This type was found on both the Witbank and Natal coalfields. They were handsome, well-proportioned British tank engines; I recorded them decked in green, red, blue and chocolate livery. All were built between 1937 and 1955. Apparently these were a modern version of the 19th century Dubs H Class 4-8-2Ts built for the Natal Government Railway but subsequently widely employed in industry.

Various South African collieries created a remarkable array of hybrids from these standard 4-8-2Ts. Springbok Colliery converted one to a 4-8-0 and added an unlikely looking, home-made, four-wheel tender.

Removal of the side tanks was necessary because water leakage created a wet rail and caused slipping. But conversely the removal of the tanks reduced the adhesion and the engines still slipped. The solution was to build false splashers along the running plate on either side and to fill them with 3½ tonnes of waste steel mixed with 1½ tonnes of concrete. This restored the lost adhesion.

There was a wonderful element of surprise when exploring the South African collieries. At Saaiwater I found a lovely, gaunt, black-clad, 'Edwardian' Class 7. Here, I wandered onto the metals of the South Witbank Consolidated Mine where I discovered a Class 8. I hadn't expected to see one of these working and later that afternoon I was able to ride on the engine as it returned to the colliery. We began the heavy climb back with empties; the sun was reduced to a quickly disappearing vermilion ball, throwing the veldt into bluish-gold shadow. The sharpness of an African winter's night was beginning to be apparent, especially as the only movements I could make as I perched on top of the tender were a series of deft contortions to avoid being struck by branches that overhung the railway. Weird sounds emanated from our engine whenever she was under strain and these alarmed a flock of guinea fowl feeding in the lineside stubble. With yelping cries they rose en masse in silhouette against the muted sunset, their shapes rivalled by the blobs of exhaust exuding, unashamedly, from the Class 8.

Another favourite type with a fine vintage flavour was the ex-Natal Government Railway Dubs A Class, 4-8-2. They once numbered one hundred engines, all from Dubs Glasgow works between 1888 and 1890. I enjoyed seeing them at Grootvlei Proprietary Mine, a major gold-producing concern at Springs. The type was also found at East Daggafontein. At the time of my visit to Springs in June 1973, South Africa supplied about 70 per cent of the free world's supply of newly mined gold.

While I was at Springs I saw the As hauling gold throughout the night. African labourers rode the hopper wagons with blazing braziers made from huge barrels with holes punched in them, so cold were the winter evenings. It was a thrilling sight to watch the veteran engine clanking its wagons loaded with cream-coloured ore. Despite the romantic connotations commonly associated with this metal, its journey to its final finished state began with 19th-century steam engines. I observed many night hauls as she rolled along the rickety track from the loading shaft, bouncing cinders in all directions and followed by a string of wagons intermittently illuminated with dancing fire from braziers. One could just discern the animated expressions and umbered tones of the labourers' faces before the whole fabulous procession disappeared away through the shadowy groves of eucalyptus trees in a ghostly swirl of steam and iron laced by a shrill, piping whistle.

The former Natal Government Railway H2 Class engines were originally 4-10-2s. After being displaced from main-line operation they were relegated to shunting and secondary duties where their five coupled wheels were a disadvantage and they were converted to 4-8-2Ts.

Many passed into industrial service and some were converted to 4-8-0s or 4-8-0Ts plus tender. Transvaal Colliery had three H2s decked in green. One was named 'Flying Scotsman' and I assumed this to be after either the famous British locomotive or the train. Nothing so obvious; the colliery concerned had a former Scottish engineer whose remarkable agility on the sports field was such that his opponents referred to him as The Flying Scotsman.

At Wankie Colliery on the border with Zambia in what was then neighbouring Rhodesia, no such archaic engines existed. They sported a stud of immaculate 19D Class 4-8-2s of 1951. I quote from my diary dated Thursday 26th July 1973: "The angular shape of a green engine came into sight with flaming droplets of incandescent fuel bouncing along underneath. She was heading a long string of empties back up to No.2 colliery.

Vomiting flame, the big engine strode towards me bearing the stress until, in a frenzied cacophony of despair, she slipped. A myriad of friction sparks from the rails were promptly doused by orange-tinted jets of steam as the sanding apparatus tried to arrest the affray. As the struggle continued, flaming cinders flew upwards with incredible velocity blanching the vigour of the star-strewn sky. Like an erupting Roman candle the heavy engine found its feet at last and dug into the rails with renewed vigour. I was witnessing a 19D, one of Africa's steam greats, this one lettered 'Wankie Colliery Company Limited No.2'."

ABOVE An Afrikaner driver on the Witbank coal field

LEFT A North British Glasgow-built 4-8-4T, one of a standard type built for South Africa's coalfields

ABOVE One of the magnificent, period Rhodesia Railways 16 Class 2-8-2+2-8-2 Garratts built by Beyer Peacock of Manchester in 1929/1930 finds a new lease of life at the Transvaal Navigation Colliery in South Africa. Saturday 26th May 1973

LEFT A train load of gold ore threads across the system at Welkom in South Africa behind a North British-built 4-8-2T

One of Landau Colliery's beautiful red Class 12A, 4-8-2s prepares for a vigorous assault on the heavy bank up to the South African Railways main line

One of the standard North British 4-8-2Ts in a delightful chocolate livery, delivers coal to a power station from the adjacent New Largo Colliery in South Africa's Transvaal. Monday 4th June 1973

South Africa: Main Lines

LONG BEFORE THE SOUTH AFRICAN expedition in 1973, I had looked forward to experiencing the country's all-steam main lines; the busiest in the world apart from those in China which were inaccessible. The trunk route between Kimberly and Bloemfontein was operated entirely by 15F and 23 Class 4-8-2s with 50 trains each way per day, many of them double headed with 2,000-tonne rakes. I returned to a world of vermilion-coloured semaphore signals against deep blue skies and an environment laced with chime whistles.

Though mainly freight, passenger trains with up to 17 coaches added variety. I spent some time at Vetrivier, a watering and fire-raking point halfway along the route. I was told that locomotives take on 15 million gallons of water a month here and 1,400 tonnes of ash are shovelled out of the pits and sent to Natal for road construction. A little less interesting were the huge deposits of char, often several feet thick, along the track sides.

In Bloemfontein I met Charlie Lewis the well-known South African photographer and other enthusiasts including Charlie's wife and Chris Butcher from Rhodesia Railways. We talked into the early hours about the enormous variety of steam in South Africa and arranged to meet the next morning on top of the Koppie Karree that overlooks the most celebrated photographic location in South Africa – the sharp curve on the nine-mile climb of 1 in 100 north of Bloomfontein on the Kroonstad main line.

The following morning the sun rose into a cloudless sky and a superb photo session ensued. On exceptionally clear mornings it was possible to see the exhausts from seven approaching trains.

The line between Kimberly and De Aar was the stamping ground of the mighty 25 Class 4-8-4s. These were the responsibility of A. G. Watson, the Loco Foreman at De Aar who was widely acclaimed for the high standards of pride he built up at this all-important depot. He introduced a general policy of one man, one engine. This led to an extraordinarily high standard of cleanliness as the crews vied with each other to have the most perfectly turned out locomotives.

The line from De Aar to Beaufort West was across the Karroo Desert where all trains were in the hands of the mighty 25C Class condensing 4-8-4s. For me these were one of the highlights of the entire African tour. Their design came about because of the serious problem of obtaining water for locomotives in the Karroo. On the 25C, the exhaust steam is fed into a turbine driving a fan blower to eject gases from the smokebox. The exhaust then passes through a 16in-diameter pipe before going through an oil separator and through another turbine that drives five air intake fans situated in the tender top. The steam then passes through condensing elements situated on both sides of the tender. Due to their condensing apparatus, the 25Cs are 107½ft long. They were the largest condensing locomotives ever built and Henschels, who produced the first example in 1953 at a cost of £112,000, claimed they could run seven hundred miles without having to take on water.

They had a superb free-running engine that had roller bearings throughout. Mr. Watson told a story of one that blew away during a gale in Cape Town. The engine, that was dead, suddenly began to move. The depot foreman chased after it and stopped it by throwing chunks of wood under the wheels. Tender fans frequently broke loose from their housings and flew off into the air. 'There are several of them lying about in the desert if you want to examine one,' Mr. Watson explained.

I experienced the sheer magic of photographing the condensers in the Karroo Desert. How does one describe the wild Karroo? A place where warm, sunny days are separated from cold, inky nights by a twilight drama of black hills and purple sunsets. A treeless, stunted expanse; paradise of the Aardvark, Rock Dassie, Cape Raven and Pied Crow to begin an endless succession. Throughout the frost tinged winter days the pure blue skies were seldom interrupted by anything other than the musty umber of locomotive smoke which hung between the golden hills like a gathering storm cloud.

In June 1973 I worked extensively between Hutchinson and Three Sisters station that takes its name from a trio of strangely shaped nearby Koppies that are a noted landmark in the Karroo. Near here I made many pictures of the 25Cs passing over a boulder strewn embankment in which lived a colony of Rock Dassies. These intensely curious mammals watched me intensely and after several days I was able to recognise eight of them individually; their antics were delightful to watch during the spells between the trains.

TOP LEFT One of the Rhodesian Railway's racy looking 15th Class 4-6-4+4-6-4 Garratt at speed near Bulawayo

RIGHT 16th CR Class Pacifics, built by the North British of Glasgow, at work on the suburban trains between Port Elizabeth and Uitenhage. The trains are seen in the flood waters of the tidal Swartkops river

TOP RIGHT Uitenhage Express. No.810, an immaculate South African Railways 16CR Class Pacific takes its vengeance under sunny skies as it hustles an eleven coach Port Elizabeth to Uitenhage train near Perseverance

ABOVE A brace of South African Railway's condensing 4-8-4s draw up to the semaphores with a fires made up and blow down valves screaming. These magnificent locomotives were amongst the world's most fascinating steam survivors

East Africa

KENYA RAILWAY'S "Mountain" Class Garratts moved with the stealth and majesty of a lion. Appropriately named after the highest mountains of East Africa, they were true giants of steam, albeit that they were metre gauge. The "Mountains" worked on the line from Mombasa, on the Indian Ocean, to the Kenyan capital Nairobi, located three hundred and thirty two miles inland and five thousand feet above sea level. At Tsavo River it was possible to see "Mountains" taking water alongside elephants standing in the river bed; undeniably one of the great railway sights of the world.

The following passage is taken from my diary notes of August 1973; "After an exciting day with the "Mountains", I returned to the wooden game lodge at Voi. From the terrace I watched the sun covering the hills with a counterpane of light and shadow - azure twilight was slowly advancing. Up above, a flock of hawks was circling effortlessly, adding a gentle, rippling momentum to the evening stillness and the valley seemed to radiate an all pervading harmony. A whistle came from below as a red Garratt distantly rolled into sight, snaking its long silver box freight across the valley floor. A red backing on the engine's nameplate was just visible; this was "Mount Kilimanjaro" heading for Mombasa." There are times when Kenya comes close to the tourist brochure claim: "God's own paradise".

The class consisted of thirty four engines built by Beyer Peacock of Gorton, Manchester in 1955. They were oil fired and in full working order weighed 252 tonnes, which gave them an axle loading of twenty one tonnes, necessitating the use of 95 pound rail. The "Mountains were one of the world's largest steam locomotives and it is remarkable that East African Railways should ever have wished for anything bigger but a 374 tonne, 4-8-4+4-8-4 Garratt, with 26 tonne axle loading and little short of half as big again as the "Mountains", did reach drawing board stage. Known as the Class 61, none were actually built and diesels were, sadly, chosen as the preferred option forward.

Later that month I embarked on an amazing journey from Tabora to Mpanda in neighbouring Tanzania. Apart from serving mining interests in Mpanda the line was used to deliver water to villages en-route during the dry season. I was allocated Inspection Saloon No.89 for the three day return trip. It was Friday evening 24th August and the train was headed by 2-8-2 No.2611, built by Bagnalls of Stafford in 1952. This engine was retained on account of its 9¾ tonne axle loading for the lightly laid Mpanda branch and was the last survivor of the Tanganyika Railway's ML Class. The two hundred and seven mile journey must be one of the remotest in Africa. It ran through arid, tangled scrub infested with Tsetse flies.

I travelled footplate into the evening; each mile riding into ever wilder country. We passed remote villages where women pounded maze with poles. Soon the village fires became less until true blackness took command relieved only by the engine's orange glow on the trackside from which hyenas and foxes gazed incredulously at man's intrusion of their domain. At midnight I went back to the saloon which lurched and swayed over the rough tracks to the extent that, at times, it was difficult believe that we were still running on rails.

We arrived at Mpanda at 09.00 the next morning. There was little to bring back, four wagons of wheat, a sugar van and four empty water tanks. On the way back the driver showed me where sister engine No.2610 was buried. One wet night the soil embankment collapsed taking the engine with it. A protrusion of maroon metal was all that could be seen; the engine was buried there forever.

It was almost twilight before we reached Ugalla River, noted for its crocodiles and hippopotamus. I slept for most of the night and it was late on Sunday morning before we arrived back in Tabora. No.2611 stabled our short rake in the sidings and having got together my things, prepared to get down from the saloon as the engine trundled past on her way to the shed. A flurry of steam, a whistle, a wave and she was gone whilst all around lay the lifeless goods yard of a Tabora Sunday.

TOP Big game at Voi. One of the world's largest steam locomotives skirts the edge of the Tsavo Game Reserve in the form of East African Railway's 59 Class 4-8-2+4-8-2 Garratt No.5914 "Mount Londiai", seen heading a 1,200 tonne freight train from Mombasa on the Indian Ocean to the Kenyan capital Nairobi

BOTTOM LEFT Former East African Railway's 26 Class, 2-8-2, No.2611 heads deep into the Tanzanian interior with a Tabora to Mpanda train

BOTTOM RIGHT Nameplate of East African Railway's Mountain Class Garratt No.5928 "Mount Kilimanjaro"

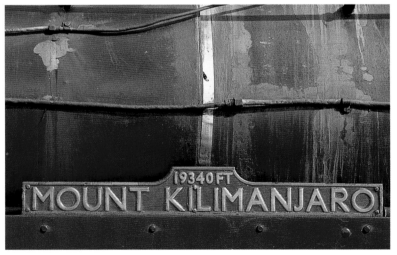

Finland - Woodburners of the Arctic Circle

MY EXPEDITION TO FINLAND in March 1972 was an eagerly awaited one, it's theme was woodburners of the Arctic Circle. I wanted to record some of Finland's last steam locomotives amid the winter snows. It was something of a grandiose vision in that relatively few woodburners still ran although many engines burnt a mixture of coal and wood. However, quite a few former woodburners still carried their spark arresting chimneys.

Finland has a distinctive family of locomotive designs many of which were built either by Tanpella or Locomo Oy. Both were based in the industrial town of Tanpella popularly referred to as the "Manchester of Finland".

The Finnish landscape is a mixture of lakes and conifer woodlands; the country possesses 60,000 lakes whilst over seventy percent of land is covered in forest. Steam had almost finished by 1972; only two hundred and fifty eight engines remained on the state railway's books, most of these were stored. Nevertheless ten different types could be seen active, albeit on shunting or permanent way trains. This was steam's last outpost in Scandinavia.

I made a base at Rovaniemi in the north a short distance from the Arctic Circle. There was an abundance of snow on the ground. The standby engine was TK3 Class 2-8-0 No.1163, complete with a large spark arresting chimney and one of a class of one hundred and sixty one engines and the most numerous Finnish type. No.1163 was called out for snow clearance duties and I was invited to help light the engine up. This was done by throwing 8 two foot long birch logs into the empty firebox after which a blazing log was added. A further ten logs were thrown in and this was sufficient to kindle the engine's fire. Several hours later, after a few more rounds of logs, the engine had sufficient steam to leave the depot and exude a sweet woody aroma.

At Rovaniemi I had an opportunity to travel footplate on Tr1 Class Mikado No.1074 on an eight hour footplate journey on an engineer's train to Raajarvi, some forty miles into Lapland. We left Rovaniemi yard at 02.41; snow was falling as I mounted No.1074's footplate. As we left Rovaniemi behind I looked from the hot, roaring locomotive to the blizzard sweeping across the desolate landscape. After some twenty minutes of extremely lively running we slowed down without warning and the driver beckoned me to his window as he waved a powerful hand torch into the snowy blackness. He found his target; there, in a beam of light was the Arctic Circle sign; we were now in Lapland and our speed rose to the engine's permitted line maximum speed limit of fifty five mph.

During the wait at Raajarvi our fireman, Mauno, demonstrated his way of making coffee by filling an ancient blackened kettle with water, hooking it onto a fire pricker and extending it into the firebox. Once boiling it was moved and ten teaspoons of ground coffee were added and the kettle left to stew, along with a couple of huge Finnish skinned sausages on the injector mount. Never did food taste so good as in that remote Lapland quarry.

Dawn broke as we returned towards Rovaniemi and the beauty of the Arctic impressed itself. Reindeer tracks could be seen alongside the railway whilst the grip of winter had rendered the many lakes and rivers invisible, their presence only being indicated by a lack of trees. With a deep throated roar our Mikado speeded its heavy train southwards flushing pairs of Willow Grouse from the lineside bushes and leaving inky blackened smoke trails across the sky.

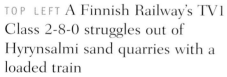 A Finnish Railway's TV1
Class 2-8-0 struggles out of
Hyrynsalmi sand quarries with a
loaded train

TOP CENTRE TV1, 2-8-0 in a
typical Finnish winter landscape

TOP RIGHT A Finnish Railways
TK3 "Jumbo" with a plain
chimney for coal burning, adds a
coach to a Helsinki bound express
at Oulu

BOTTOM A dawn scene at Raajarvi
as TR1 Class Mikado No.1074
shunts in the quarry

TOP LEFT TK3 Class 2-8-0 No.1165, built by A/S Frichs in 1949, shunts at Oulu on Saturday 25th March 1972 under the watchful gaze of four passing cyclists

TOP RIGHT Finnish Tr1 Mikado No.1074 crosses the Arctic Circle on its return to Rovaniemi from Raagarvi on Tuesday 28th March 1972

BOTTOM Spring thaw; as winter relaxes its icy grip on Finland's rivers, a TV1 Class 2-8-0 ambles towards Kontiomaki with a freight from Hyrynsalmi

The Incredible Stone Railway, Sumatra

THE MOST REMARKABLE aspect of north Sumatra's great steam hunting ground was the stone carrying railway based at Gunung Kataren. I reached it by the Siantar Express bus and whoever named it that wasn't joking; during the journey the horn blared continuously as the vehicle was aimed along narrow, congested roads at breakneck speed. The bus was packed solid, including passengers on the roof, and the journey was further enlivened by rollicking music which blared out continuously from its cracked speakers.

My destination was located in the middle of a dense forest and following a rough track through the trees I eventually reached a primitive stone crusher alongside which, at the head of a string of diminutive wagons, stood engine No.106, a Dutch built 0-6-0 from Ducroo and Brauns of Weesp. The engine was about to return with empties and, with no formalities, I jumped into the cab and soon we were shuffling along rickety tracks which passed trees laden with bananas. After two miles we stopped at the top of an enormous rope worked incline. Looking down I could see the line continued through even denser forests. I climbed down the precarious slope and reaching the bottom of the incline had little time to wait before the train which worked the lower section appeared in the form of engine No.105, a well tank built by Orenstein and Koppel in 1920. In the instant, I spotted an anomaly which could not be explained; the stones in the wagons had not been quarried, they were round and smooth! Communications were impossible so,

once again, I climbed aboard the engine and waited for it to return with the empties. No.105 rasped, snorted and clanked it's way through the forest, riding like a wild horse, the engine's huge chimney constantly clouting the overhanging vegetation and sending shrouds of foliage spinning in all directions. After a couple of miles or so the line ended on the bank of a wide river and alongside were several native rafts from which stones were being unloaded. There was no quarry! The stones were being gathered from the river bed by natives diving off rafts. About a hundred stones was the maximum each boat would hold without risk of sinking whereupon they came to the river bank and the stones were manually loaded into the wagons from wicker baskets.

I travelled back with the loaded train and upon reaching the incline it became apparent that the engine was precariously low on water. There was some panic and two buckets were flung from the cab and one man, bucket in hand, dashed into the undergrowth and jumped into a boggy spring two feet deep. A small human chain of labourers juggled with the buckets which were full when they left the spring but half empty before they reached the man sitting astride the engine filling the tank.

I had never witnessed so Heath Robinson a railway but it was not some remote industrial concern; it was operated by the Indonesian State Railway and was, apparently, an important source of ballast for the main line network.

The Indonesian State Railways sixty centimetre gauge stone railway in northern Sumatra was a haven of antiquity in every respect. Here, Orenstein and Koppel 0-6-0T No.105 is seen approaching the cable operated incline with a train load of stones from the river

One of Indonesian State Railways'
many delightful antiquities was
this D15 Class 0-8-0T, the last
survivor of its type. Here the
veteran receives attention at Cepu
Depot in northern Java

Java Main Line

AS RECENTLY AS THE 1970S Java's main-line railway system was like a vast working museum. Eight hundred 3ft 6in-gauge steam locomotives were on the books of the Indonesian State Railway, although only half of them would be active at any one time and some were permanently derelict. An incredible 65 different classes were included, many of 19th century origin. Other forms could be traced back to the earliest days of railways.

If the Javan sugar plantation locomotives were added, the island would have had something like 1,500 locomotives in hundreds of different designs. For an unassuming tropical island like Java that is only six hundred miles long and less than a hundred miles wide, these amazing statistics create a kind of Galapagos.

It was popularly believed that the 2-4-0 passenger engine was extinct until a batch was discovered working a secondary line in Java. Classified B50, they were introduced from Sharp Stewart's works on Great Bridgewater Street, Manchester, in 1880 – seven years before the company moved to Glasgow!

There were also some vintage 2-4-0Ts, classified B13, that had come from the German builder Hanomag as long ago as 1885.

The island abounded in 19th century-built steam trams that, in the Dutch tradition, worked on roadside tramways. Some of these engines were built by Beyer Peacock. The C11 2-6-0 type, built by Hartmann of Chemnitz, was a classic period piece that dated back to 1879.

The island also had some standard-gauge locomotives. At Balakarga Works, in Jogjakarta, lay the world's last 0-4-2 express passenger engines. There were four here that were built by Beyer Peacock in the early 1880s. These engines were left behind following the Japanese invasion of Java in 1942 when the island's standard-gauge railway equipment was looted and taken to Manchuria where the retreating Chinese had dismantled the railway.

Also in the Jogjakarta dump was a Beyer Peacock outside-frame goods engine of 1885, a gem that bore more than a hint of Kirtley's numerous 0-6-0s of the Midland Railway produced between 1863 and 1874. The 0-4-2, along with its more prolific relation the 2-4-0, evolved in Britain during the 1830s.

Although it was the vintage engines that made Java most famous, it had numerous other delights still active including Skirt Tanks; Prussian style 4-4-0 express passenger engines; beautiful C53 Class compound Pacifics by Werkspoor of Amsterdam; beautifully proportioned German and Dutch built 4-6-4Ts; imposing Klien Linder 0-8-0s; 2-12-2Ts that, although massive, fell well short of the mighty Alco-built DD51 Class 2-8-8-0 Mallets that slogged up the 1-in-40 grades of the volcanic uplands between Tasikmalaja and Citjalengka on the Jakarta to Surabaya main line.

It need hardly be mentioned that nothing remains of this treasure house today.

FAR LEFT An Indonesian railway's B50 class 2-4-0 heads an early morning passenger train from Madiun to Ponorogo

LEFT An Indonesian railway's C12 class 2 cylinder compound 2-6-0 T

The Insular Lumber Company's
awesome 0-6-6-0 four-cylinder
compound Mallet threads a rake
of freshly cut mahogany across
the Maaslud Viaduct en route to
the coastal saw mill at Fabrica

Philippines, Insular Lumber, a Legend

CONRADO EMERGED FROM the telephone office and standing outlined against the light streaming through the door, he called 'No.7's within two kilometres'. This message heralded the end of a three-hour wait in the Insular Lumber Company's coastal saw mill at Fabrica on the Philippine island of Negros. No.7 was the world's most incredible steam survivor. The three hours were incidental since I had waited years to see this engine; years accompanied by the fear that it might be withdrawn. At last the moment of truth had arrived. The crossing gates over the Bacolod-Sagay Road rattled down as a distant whistle rang out like a cold shiver. The enormous, mahogany-burning Mallet – twice as large as I had imagined – eased herself, tender first, over the crossing. I was spellbound by the disjointed and freakish conglomeration of locomotion. She was unique! The crossing lights revealed her faded green livery lined in red although her ornate eight-wheeled bogie tender was done in black with white letters pronouncing with abandon 'Insular Lumber Company', lesser scripts beneath proclaimed 'No riders allowed'.

With mahogany sparks curling from her smoke stack and rasping steam from all cylinders, she clanked past with a long trainload of log cars piled high with trunks eerily gliding after her into the gloom. She stopped at the saw mill on a ledge high above a huge artificial lake. The logs were to be pushed mechanically from the wagons and allowed to crash violently down a slope into the water below known as the log pan. From here the conveyer took them to the saw mill, the logs being easier to process when wet.

On the opposite side of the lake I watched No.7 ease a log car into position and, after grappling with it for a few seconds, the pusher dislodged an enormous trunk and sent it thundering down into the pan. The ground shook under the impetus and when the log finally hit the lake it sent a terrific spray of water some 40 feet skywards. With three trunks sent down in rapid succession, No.7 drew her wagons forwards emitting grotesque sounds from her four leaking cylinders, all with their valves out of alignment. Like an anguished creature she moved forward

and, back lit by sodium light from the mill, her acrid silhouette seemed to be ever changing in ghostly patterns amid fire and swirling steam.

After all the logs had been ejected, she pushed the cars out of the mill. Each slip of a wheel obscured her in steam and produced a jet of crimson sparks accompanied by the most hideous sounds ever emitted from a locomotive. Never had I heard or imagined an engine so haunted; the hollow rasps of her uneven exhaust might have been a ghost howling in hell.

Conrado Gabrial was the company's engineer and he confirmed that No.7 had a long, strange history.

'That engine has been involved in more accidents and deaths than I care to remember,' he said. 'One of the worst was one night after heavy rains when No.7 started off a huge landslide as she rounded a hill. Thousands of tonnes of rock gave way under her and she rolled into a completely irretrievable position in a river bed far below. The Mallet had to be dismantled where she lay and the pieces hauled back up to track level by winching ropes. The wires used can still be found to this day on the overgrown hillside'.

It was October 1974 and I had dreamed of photographing No.7 with one of Insular Lumber's vertical-cylinder Shays side by side in the dead of night spraying the tropical vegetation with fire. It was an image I saw in my imagination long before I reached that enchanted island. To that end I moved up to base camp at Minapasuk. Here the Shays plied logs from the loading area to the exchange sidings at Maaslud for the big Mallet to take them over precarious metals down to the saw mill at coast level. The 21-mile journey took about six hours because of frequent derailments, and the maximum speed was 10mph!

Base camp was a real backwoods community, isolated and delightfully hospitable, a place where the aroma of wood smoke drifting from the Shays mingled with the fragrance of native-brewed coffee stewing in wooded eating houses by the wayside. Logging is rough and dangerous work; accidents, derailments and mechanical problems assume nightmare proportions and the men, warm as they are in disposition, inevitably have acquired an aura of ruggedness.

During my time at base camp a typhoon struck and the rain lashed down for two whole days. The track disappeared under a sea of mud yet the indomitable Shays, with all the pugnacity endorsed by their appearance, unstintingly went about their duties and continued whirring their way along at full throttle maintaining the usual 10mph.

When the rain finally stopped I ventured up to the loading area. The green-clad mountains were bathed in a twilight mist and the huge trunks were piled up in a tangled mass starkly contrasting with the lifting gear. Standing in a quagmire of mud I watched the twilight deepen and listened to the melodious whistle cry of Shay No.12 on her way up from Maaslud. A chattering flurry

from her pounding cylinders finally broke the silence as her bizarre shape emerged through the mist beneath a swirl of fire.

The loaded trains left Maaslud behind No.7 and within half a mile crossed over the wooden-trestled viaduct built under American colonial rule in the finest of wild-west traditions. This was a definitive location, No.7's tender was piled high with mahogany off-cuts and an active volcano in the background completed a classic scene.

Although virile, the antiquarians of Insular Lumber had little time to operate and on my return to Negros seven years later to make the film 'The Dragons of Sugar Island' for the BBC, I found Mallet No.7 and Shay No.12 dumped and rusted. No longer would these two dinosaurs spray the vegetation with fire. Now that vegetation grew through every chink and crevice of their iron work.

Spraying the tropical vegetation with fire, Insular Lumber Company's Mallet No.7 with three-truck vertical-cylinder Shay No.12 from Lima of Ohio. This scene from the 1974 expedition contrasts with the picture that shows how I found them in 1981 when I returned to the Philippines to make 'The Dragons of Sugar Island' in the BBC's 'Great Little Railways' series

FAR LEFT Lima three-truck Shay No.12 of the Insular Lumber Company shuffles between the Maaslud exchange and the loading area in the early hours of the morning in October 1974

LEFT Colouring the night sky with fire, Shay No.10 of the Insular Lumber Company shuffles between the saw mill and the planing mill at Fabrica

BELOW Dome and whistle, sandbox and spark-arresting chimney of one of Insular Lumber Company's Shays at sunrise in Fabrica

Philippines, Dragons of Sugar Island

MY SOUTHEAST ASIAN expedition of summer 1974 was amazing by any standards. It concentrated on the vintage types surviving in Java and Sumatra along with the array of American engines working on Negros island in the Philippines. 'Iron Dinosaurs,' my book about the expedition, attracted much attention including that of the BBC when planning their 'Great Little Railways' series.

Following a meeting with BBC TV in Manchester, it was agreed that a film based on the book should be made called 'The Dragons of Sugar Island' and that I would return to Negros with producer Derek Towers to prepare the script and shooting sequences.

Derek had no particular interest in railways and apart from gleaning a flavour of Negros from 'Iron Dinosaurs', he was relying on my local knowledge and contacts.

Accordingly, the two of us visited the island in December 1981 for a three-week recce in readiness for the film crew who would follow in January.

It was a hectic three weeks. We visited all the sugar mills and made contact with people I had worked with while compiling material for 'Iron Dinosaurs' seven years previously. We returned to Britain just before Christmas but it was a short break for Derek who went back with the film crew in January while I stayed in Britain to write the narrative and prepared to record it as soon as the film was made.

I was pleased with the result, it was a new experience to see some of my still pictures come to life. The film opens with the primeval feel of moonlight scenes across a lagoon, swaying palms silhouetted against the sky and tropical sounds that pierce the stillness.

Suddenly this atmosphere is broken by a strange, off-beat panting sound and a swirling ball of fire becomes visible, getting larger as the weird sound increases.

Ostensibly it is a dragon. At this stage the identity of the fire-throwing beast remains tantalisingly obscure until the bizarre form of Mao Central's No.5, a battered, hybridised, American Mogul of 1924, becomes discernible in the moonlight throwing a column of crimson fire 20ft into the air as she storms towards the camera. Amid swirling steam and fire the apparition heads away into the darkness, arched by two palm trees through which a watery dawn is breaking.

This amazing sequence was almost certainly the first time a fire-throwing steam locomotive had appeared on moving film. The technicalities involved in achieving this were tremendous but the sequence is a perfect depiction of how engines that burn straw-like cane waste actually appear when working hard at night.

Gangs of men armed with knives emerge in the early light as they leave their bamboo villages and head for surrounding fields of sugar cane. The work is hard, back-breaking and monotonous. Apart from the vicious strokes needed to cut the cane, there is the constant hazard of razor-sharp leaves and thorns that jag into the flesh of all but the most experienced workers. The moisture-laden cane is as heavy as mahogany and each worker has to cut ten tonnes a shift to receive the pittance of 90p a day.

The film then follows a carabao, or water buffalo, trundling its way to the railhead with a cart piled high with cane. Its arrival coincides with Hawaiian Philippine Company's 'Dragon No.6'. We watch the engine prepare a long rake of loaded cane and then follow it in a series of long shots through the landscape to music specially composed by Harold Davidson. The film makes a dramatic contrast with the wasteful, dangerous and environmentally destructive road system where overloaded cane lorries lie upside down and half the occupants of the island's hospitals are victims of the roads.

The serious problems of the sugar industry are fully explored, in particular the fall in world prices caused in part by the Common Market dumping its surplus production onto the world market. The sugar industry's decline has had a dramatic effect on the island's population.

But the situation in the villages pales to insignificance when compared with the plight of the Sacadas. This is the name given to the migrant workers who come with their families from neighbouring islands to cut the cane during the season. The film shows an open-plan compound where over two hundred of these itinerants live in appalling squalour. As the men labour in the fields

heir women and children remain listlessly in the
ompounds. The Sacadas' diet consists of rice and dried
sh supplemented by sugar cane that supplies an
nstant source of energy to keep the pangs of hunger at
ay. Malnutrition was even more rife here than in the
illages because the Sacadas are open to exploitation by
he contractors who hire them out to landowners. To
itness their deprivation was a shattering and harrowing
xperience. In these tragic places, men with the
ughest constitutions cry tears of anguish at their lot
nd the poignancy of the situation is reflected in bitter,
ark music.

This brings us to one of the film's most breathtaking
moments when one of the Sacadas begins to play a
uitar with all the potency of a southern blues. The
nger accompanies him in native Cebuano but the
anguage is irrelevant because the music speaks from
he soul. The camera moves slowly from the musicians
o the people lying around the compound, their haunted
xpressions resembling the occupants of a Breughal
ainting; a baby suckles a woman's breast, a ragged child
naws on a stick of cane and a one-legged man hobbles
ith amazing rapidity across the yard. The song is about
Cebu, an adjacent island where most of these poor souls
nce lived.

The supercharged atmosphere is finally relieved by a
whistle's screech as 'Mao No.1', a battered Mogul of
lassic American proportions, charges across a bridge

spanning a river in which a group of carabaos are lying
almost completely submerged.

One of the great disappointments of the second
expedition was that the Insular Lumber Company's
compound Mallet and vertical-cylinder Shays that were
featured extensively in 'Iron Dinosaurs', were no longer
working. We did include them lying derelict but the film
was visually the poorer for not showing them in action.

However, I did arrange for Conrado Gabrial, the
former Locomotive Superintendent of the Insular
Lumber Company, to talk to camera about railroading
on Negros.

Conrado, who I had worked with extensively in 1974,
was a superb individual. He had the aura of Bunk
Johnson and looked like Anthony Quinn.

There follows a slow dissolve from Conrado to the
whirring cylinders of a Shay and from the interior of a
firebox through to shimmering white smoke as Hawaiian
Philippine's 'Dragon No.9' approaches through a field of
burning stubble. As the dragon moves up through the
smoke, two children are seen running along the track
hand in hand. The engine's whistle rings out above the
blazing inferno. The burning stubble signified the end of
the season and so the cycle begins again, as it must if
the island is to survive.

For all its social and economic problems one thing is
certain; when the dragons finally become extinct, Sugar
Island will never be the same again.

BELOW TOP Manual loading of sugar-cane wagons

BELOW CENTRE A Carabao arrives at the rail head with a cart load of sugar on the Ma Ao network

BOTTOM Hawaiian Philippine Company's 'Dragon No.6'

BOTTOM LEFT One of the Hawaiian Philippine Company's delightful 'Dragons' on Negros island

RIGHT Ma Ao Sugar Central's No.1, an Alco 2-6-0, heads a night train along the Cut Cut line on Saturday 2nd November 1974

FAR RIGHT Hawaiian Philippine Company's 'Dragon No.6' in blue livery with stove pipe chimney for oil burning

BELOW Battered Alco Mogul No.3 of the Ma Ao Sugar Central with a tender piled high with bales of bagasse

The Little Fireless of Schwertberg, Austria

IN THE DAYS of main-line steam, it was easy to overlook industrial systems and especially the Fireless locomotives that might be found in such environments. These engines had no fire in their bellies and were relatively inanimate. Also they seldom went very far because they were dependent on a ready supply of high-pressure steam. But in many respects, the Fireless was the most efficient and economical shunting unit ever devised. Only a driver was required, there was little to go wrong, they were cheap to produce and ideal for those industries where sparks from a conventional engine would wreak havoc, such as paper mills and ammunition factories.

Fireless engines came in a remarkable variety of guises that has led to them becoming the subject of a fascinating global study.

The most interesting example I have located was the Little Fireless of Schwertberg whose job it was to take 600mm-gauge wagons of prepared clay from the Schwertberg works of Kamig AG in northern Austria to the standard-gauge connection with the Austrian State Railways' St. Valentin to Krems line. Built by Floridsdorf of Vienna in 1930, the engine was unusual in sallying forth down a branch line.

Although Fireless engines are often thought of as Thermos flasks on wheels, the Schwertberg engine was known locally as the Wursteldampfer, that means sausage heater or hot dog machine. The Kamig plant opened in 1922 and used horses to convey prepared clay until the Fireless arrived, and when rails were laid they followed the same route in the manner of a roadside tramway.

The accompanying picture was taken on Wednesday 8th September 1976 and shows the engine's driver who had worked on it for 22 years. Despite its efficiency, he said that derailments or icy rails invariably could be relied upon to deposit the engine in an embarrassing position and the problems of returning it to the factory without steam were legion.

The driver also described the night the engine ran away. It was during the late shift; the engine had been filled in readiness for a trip but when the crew came to take the train out, the engine had gone. Pandemonium broke loose, the sidings were searched to no effect. The engine was not in the factory. A search of the line was made but she had vanished into thin air. A panic-stricken phone call to the village established that the engine had passed through half an hour previously, narrowly missing a car, but no one had realised that the engine was not manned. The train crew, along with a fitter, set off for the exchange sidings horrified by what they might discover.

For five minutes lamps flashed around the darkened sidings until in a far away corner up against a mound of earth there she stood like 'The Titfield Thunderbolt' itself. Though none the worse for wear, the steam pressure had fallen too low to return the engine to the factory. Small wonder every one gave it up that night and made for the nearest ale house.

Kamig AG's Fireless engine heads a rake of prepared clay down to the exchange sidings with the Austrian State Railways

Pakistan – British Thoroughbreds

BRITAIN WAS THE RAILWAY BUILDER to an empire and to the world so it was fitting that two of Britain's definitive forms of locomotive should end their days working in the remoteness of The Punjab. At Malakwal Junction both the inside-cylinder 0-6-0 and inside-cylinder 4-4-0 could be found. The former was the British trusty maid of all work and a form of engine built continuously from the 1830s until the 1940s.

The inside cylinder 4-4-0 was a principal express passenger type of late Victorian and Edwardian Britain. These two forms of locomotive, often with interchangeable boilers, appeared in many manifestations. Most of Britain's home railways possessed them and although the dimensions of many designs were similar, each company produced them in their own family likeness.

The inside-cylinder 0-6-0 was the mainstay of British freight haulers throughout the 19th century and into the 20th too. As late as the 1960s it could still be seen occasionally on main-line freight consists. Following their replacement in main-line service they frequently gravitated to the shunting yards.

Britain's most numerous steam type was Ramsbottom's London and North Western DX inside-cylinder 0-6-0s that totalled 947 examples. The Midland Railway produced inside-cylinder 0-6-0s continuously and in huge numbers, like the sorcerer's apprentice who couldn't stop making broomsticks. And if one engine were insufficiently powerful for a given duty, two would be provided.

The inside-cylinder 4-4-0 was of an equally noble lineage, although the first were not built until the 1870s. Their wheel configuration was a particularly elegant and harmonious one and this symmetry enabled appearance-conscious designers of the late Victorian and Edwardian period to produce some startlingly beautiful designs. Along with their inside-cylinder 0-6-0 relations, the two types formed the mainstay of motive power on many railways well into the 20th century.

Although widely used in Britain, the two forms appeared relatively sparsely in export packages. The Indian sub-continent was a notable exception and under the BESA locomotive standardisation programme of 1903, both types were included in a set of designs for the 5ft 6in-gauge lines of the sub-continent.

In January 1977 I arrived in Malakwal having travelled overnight from Lahore. Accommodation was provided in the railway guest house opposite the loco shed. Traffic was busy and it was an emotional experience to see once again the type of locomotives I had been brought up with in Britain.

The Pakistan Railway SGS Class inside-cylinder 0-6-0s were very similar to Robinson's Great Central Railway 'Pom Poms' of 1901, while the SPS inside-cylinder 4-4-0s bore more than a hint of the Manchester Sheffield and Lincolnshire Railway styling.

The railway was not run easily, shortages of locomotives, spares and rolling stock caused some trains to be cancelled and provided a constant headache for the operators. But I was looked after superbly, the guest house was comfortable and warm with a roaring log fire. Hot water was provided in buckets, having been taken from the injector overflow pipe of the nearest engine.

After a few days I realised that there was a severe shortage of fuel in the Punjab. Mahboob Rabbani, the Assistant Mechanical Engineer, and Abdul Razzaq, the Head Train Examiner along with their assistants, were having their daily operational meetings in unheated rooms either at the station or over at the shed. I insisted that they used the guest-house fuel but they wouldn't hear of it. Eventually a compromise was reached and subsequently they conducted their meetings in the warmth of the guest house. These crisis sessions often went on very late into the night and were conducted as I sat alongside writing up my notes and my photography record book.

Eleven glorious days were spent at Malakwal. The SPSs emitted a musical plonk from their side rods just as I remember the Midland Railway Simples doing when I was a small boy. And like the former Great Central 'Pom Poms', the SGSs had a superb explosive exhaust beat, especially when drawing their heavy trains away from the yard.

ABOVE A tribesman and his camel wait patiently for a Pakistan Railways' inside-cylinder 0-6-0 to draw its 63-wagon consist out of the yard at Paktowel. The engine is seen heading a trans-Punjab freight from Malakwal to Shorkot

FAR LEFT The definitive 'Manchester' engine in the form of Pakistan Railways' SPS Class 4-4-0 heads away from Malakwal

LEFT A British-built inside-cylinder 0-6-0 heads a freight train from Paktowel in the Pakistani Punjab

ABOVE A Pakistan Railways' SPS Class inside-cylinder 4-4-0 and an Indian Railways' standard XA Light Pacific bask in the golden evening sunlight at Malakwal loco shed in the Punjab

TOP RIGHT A standard Indian Railways' XA Class Light Pacific at Malakwal

RIGHT A Pakistan Railways' inside-cylinder 0-6-0 at Malakwal in the Punjab

Breaker's Yards, India

'Gone now the clanging shovel; gone the sweet sooty emanations of oil and steam; gone the living spirit of man's most animated machine. Gone to a jigsaw in iron and steel are those whose wheels have come full circle.'

AT THE BEGINNING OF 1981 a directive came from the Chairman of the Railway Board in Delhi that condemned all non-standard steam locomotives throughout India. This had been brought about by the freeing up of large numbers of WG Class Mikados from lines already dieselised or electrified. It was a shock because the older British designs were, until then, being phased out slowly. India's 5ft 6in-gauge lines would look very sparse with only three standard types in operation; WP, WG and CWD.

Most locomotives in India were broken up randomly, often in sidings alongside depots. Sometimes the scrap contractors' men would encamp alongside the engines and live on the site for days or even weeks while the work was being done. My first experience of India's scrapyards was in October 1976 at Shakurbasti near Delhi where SGC Class No.36644 – Vulcan Foundry 1912 – was on the scrap line. The following month I visited Sultanpur breaker's yard near Lucknow where many BESA inside-cylinder 0-6-0s were being broken up.

However, many engines did go to Jamalpur Works for scrapping and here there were several sidings in which condemned engines were placed. I spent a week in Jamalpur in March 1981 living in an inspector's saloon alongside the station. It was a time when dozens of British steam locomotives were arriving to be broken up including the XC Pacifics, the last high-speed British locomotives left on earth. On Wednesday 18th March 1981, four XCs were auctioned and a further eight arrived. Once auctioned the engines were taken to the scraping bays but cutting up did not begin until the contractor's money had been deposited in the railway's bank account.

It was ironical that I had been at Jamalpur in December 1976 when the mighty, related XE Mikados were being withdrawn from the eastern coalfield, many having been allocated to Asansol.

For some half century these giants had hauled 1,500-tonne coal trains over the hilly regions of Bengal between Asansol and Jha Jha. The XEs were hauled into the yard by the scrapyard pilot, SGC Class 0-6-0 No.34225, a Vulcan Foundry engine of 1920.

I recorded the cutting up of XE No.22543, built on the river Clyde by Beardmore of Dalmuir in the 1930s. Over two days this magnificent locomotive was reduced to an enormous pile of scrap. Labourers manually hacked off the boiler rivet heads, 20 vicious, back-breaking blows being needed to remove each one. The foreground was dominated by aspects of the subject's anatomy; a crank axle, dome cover, piston, chimney, cylinder valves, driving-wheel fragments, springs and a buffer.

RIGHT AND TOP RIGHT Breaking up Indian Railways XE Class Mikados at Jamalpur Works in December 1976

CENTRE RIGHT An Indian Railways SGS Class being cut up at Sultanpur on 6th November 1976

BOTTOM RIGHT The last sunset; Indian Railways last surviving GC1 Class 2-8-0 being broken up at Jamalpur Works

RIGHT Cabside detail from an SGS-Class locomotive allocated to Lucknow and broken up at Sultanpur in November 1976

India – Incredible Bagnalls

A DOCTOR FROM DIBRUGARH hunting in the dense jungles of Upper Assam discovered coal fragments in a river bed. He subsequently brought two geologists from Britain and large quantities of high quality coal were discovered. This gave rise to the collieries, tea gardens and timber industries of Upper Assam that were developed in the 1890s by the Assam Railway Trading Company. The coalfield was close to the border with Burma and China.

From the outset, the company chose 2ft-gauge saddle tanks of a standard design from Bagnalls of Stafford and the first two examples arrived in 1894, one for the coalfield and one for the Jokai Tea Company; this engine was named 'Pekoe Tip'. Assam tea was to become universally acclaimed for its full-bodied flavour. In all, 15 Bagnall saddle tanks went to Assam between 1894 and 1931. Some were 0-4-2s others 0-4-0s with cylinder sizes ranging between five and seven inches.

By the time of my first visit in November 1976, the entire coalfield evoked a feeling reminiscent of early industrial times in Britain; a place where time had stood still. Most of the coal output was for use in Assam as the field is extremely remote and high transport costs to most of India have ensured that operations remain modest both in output and thinking. The colliery and slag tips co-exist with the workers' tiny dwellings around which ragged children play. In the evenings, the valleys were shrouded in a smoky haze caused by the fires of the dwellings.

The smoking boiler house chimneys of the collieries, starkly silhouetted against the hills and locomotive sounds, day and night, gave piquancy to a pristine industrial landscape.

A brickworks, complete with a Manchester kiln was built at Ledo to provide brick linings for the collieries. The clay was brought from the surrounding pits by rail; two Bagnalls being assigned for the purpose. The clay was hacked from the earth by colourfully dressed women, loaded into wicker baskets and carried on the women's heads before being loaded manually into the diminutive four-wheeled tubs of the waiting train. The operation resembled a scene that could have been seen in rural Wales at the dawn of the industrial revolution.

At Ledo Brickworks I descended narrow, coal-begrimed steps down to a Lancashire boiler set in the bowels of the works, it was like walking backwards in time. The shadowy, crumbling wall flickered with crimson fire glow and amid the dancing shadows flitted the ghosts of Watt and Trevithick. One might have expected Trevithick to emerge, spanner in hand, from the stationary engine house where the ground and walls pulsated with the pounding motion of the huge engine that, with rhythmic rasps of steam, drove the Archimedean screw.

This compacted the newly delivered clay that emerged in huge blocks to be cut manually into brick shapes with a huge cutter, rather like cutting portions from a block of cheese. The raw bricks were then taken to a Manchester Kiln to be cooked before final steam drying, the heating being supplied from a second Lancashire boiler located next to the one that drove the engine.

Small gangs of gaily dressed women carried slack to the boiler houses in wicker baskets on their heads. The slack was then emptied through holes in the floor into the acrid, sulphurous Manchester Kiln that raged below.

At Namdang Colliery a Lancashire boiler lifted up the coals from the mine via an inclined plane. At Tirap mine I found 'David', a particularly decrepit 0-4-0 of 1924. The engine had no cab and the working pressure had been reduced by half because of the boiler's poor condition. 'David' was dragging his wagons around with a chain and clearly looked to be on his last legs, pulling only half the wagons he could in his prime.

Almost 23 years were to elapse before I returned to the Assam coalfield in January 1999. This time I flew from Calcutta to Dibrugarh and, having crossed the waterways of Bangladesh, I continued due eastwards following the course of the mighty Brahmaputra river. It was a breathtakingly beautiful journey and I thought of the British pioneers who had set sail from Calcutta in Scottish-built paddle steamers, plied their way up through the rivers of what is now Bangladesh and entered the mighty Brahmaputra to sail eastwards, into the inhospitable, leech-ridden jungles of Upper Assam. It was a distance of approximately a thousand miles that, with stops, took 28 days.

Predictably the activity on the coalfield was very much less than before. Some of the mines had closed, including Namdang and its inclined plane lay derelict. But Ledo Brickworks was still in operation with two Bagnalls, one of which, incredibly, was 'David' that was not just working, but recently back from Margherita Works where it had received a major overhaul – although the cab was still missing! The other engine was not identifiable, having evolved from numerous spare parts of withdrawn sisters. The two locomotives were continuing a 105-year tradition of Bagnalls working on the Assam coalfield.

Ledo Brickworks was steeped in the history of a bygone industrial age and some of the scenes that confronted me resembled drawings by Lowry. It was, without doubt, a classic industrial landscape and the most visually powerful I had ever seen.

The only colliery that remained steam operated was Tirap, reached after a 25-mile journey over the unmade Stilwell Road, along which the allied troops invaded Burma during World War Two. The route was named after General Stilwell of the US Army or 'Vinegar Joe' as he was popularly known. Tirap had dispensed with its Bagnalls and operated three ex-Darjeeling and Himalayan Railway 0-4-0STs that had been built to a design by Sharp Stewart of Glasgow in 1880.

During my ten-day stay I lived in the guest house at Tirap and on most days commuted along the Stilwell Road to Ledo. I worked hard to make the best of the scenes that surrounded me. I would never see their likes again.

However, despite all my scripting and planning, the definitive picture of that coalfield came during the last 40 minutes of my visit. I was waiting at Ledo for a vehicle to come down from Tirap to take me back to Margherita when the unidentified Bagnall left the works with empties bound for the clay pit.

Everything was right: the light, the smoke, the open fire door of the engine, the pile of freshly made orange bricks in the foreground, the smoking works chimney and the distant slag tips laced in golden light. They all combined to produce a scene that totally captured the uniqueness of that amazing coalfield.

ABOVE 'David' fresh from an overhaul at Margherita Works, awaits his next turn of duty at Ledo Brickworks, Upper Assam

LOWER RIGHT The crew of the unidentified Bagnall 0-4-0STY at Ledo Brickworks in February 1999.

UPPER RIGHT 'Ram Ring', Bagnall 0-4-0STY No.1733 of 1904, delivers coals to the Lancashire boiler house at Namdang Colliery on the Assam coalfield on 28th November 1976. The driver was photographed almost 23 years later during my 1999 expedition to Assam standing in exactly the same position! See picture below

In the Ledo Brickworks clay pits gaily dressed women hack clay from the earth and load it onto the waiting train. The engine was one of Assam coalfield's 0-4-2STs but the trailing axle has long gone. Unnamed when pictured, it was originally 'Takaur', No.1556 of 1899

Photographed on Saturday 20th November 1976, more gangs of gaily dressed women fill their wicker baskets with slack that eventually will be emptied into the Manchester kiln at the Ledo Brickworks

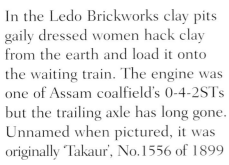

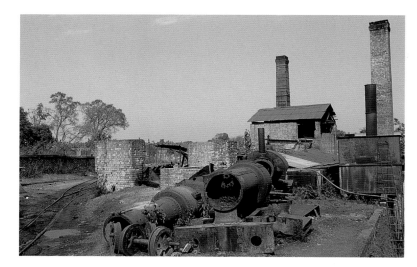

ABOVE Two Bagnalls were working at Ledo Brickworks in 1999 and both are seen here in the loco shed area at the top end of the works. In front is 'David' and behind is the unidentified sister engine that had been assembled from parts of other condemned locomotives

TOP LEFT An amazing scene of industrial antiquity at Ledo Brickworks in February 1999. The remains of condemned Bagnall saddle tanks lie in the foreground

LEFT This picture was made during the last 40 minutes of my visit to Ledo Brickworks in February 1999. It says everything I would wish to express about this remarkable place. I cannot imagine ever making a better picture of an industrial steam locomotive

Bengal Industry

INDIA'S EASTERN COALFIELD in Bengal gave rise to a superb range of industries and well into the 1970s a variety of British locomotives remained in action, both in the form of main line and industrial types. One of the largest fleets of industrial locomotives was at Calcutta Port Trust where 45 heavy duty 0-6-2Ts that were built between 1945 and 1954 by Hunslet and Mitsubishi, could be found.

Indian Iron and Steel's Burnpur works and Kulti Iron Works, both near Asansol, were, in common with the main-line network, built during the British period and it was fitting that definitive British industrial designs should proliferate. The roster embraced Andrew Barclay 0-4-0STs and 0-6-0STs; Hawthorn Leslie 0-6-0STs and 0-6-0Ts; Nasmyth Wilson 2-6-0Ts and Robert Stephenson and Hawthorn 0-4-0STs and 0-6-0Ts. The iron ore for these and other Indian iron and steel plants came from the vast deposits at Manoharpur in Bihar where a stud of Andrew Barclay 0-4-2To operated.

One of the saddest omissions of my documentation of the 'Last Steam Locomotives of the World' was the failure to cover the industrial landscape of the Bengal coalfield in the Dhanbad and Asansol areas. Many branches left the main line to service the surrounding collieries whose winding gear and smoking chimneys stood out starkly in the industrial environment. Many of these lines were formally worked by British HT Class 2-8-2Ts or BESA-designed 2-8-0s until WGs took over. Because I was pursuing older British designs I left the coalfields with their WG operations until last. Consequently, the following was the situation on India's Eastern Railway on the 16th February 1981 when I arrived in Calcutta at 06.15am on the Kalka Mail:

XE Asansol	All condemned
XC Burdwan	8 in service, all to be withdrawn by the summer
HT, 2-8-2To	Auctioned, currently being broken up
HGS, 2-8-0s	4 survivors, to be withdrawn after CWD replacements. Modified with lower chimneys for restricted workings
WM Class, 2-6-4To	Disappearing rapidly
SGC/SGS, 0-6-0s	All but extinct

I never got back to those colliery branches and still think about them all these years later, especially now that such environments are all but extinct.

Although these deficiencies sadden me, in truth there never was going to be sufficient time to do everything that had to be done.

RIGHT A Robert Stephenson and Hawthorn 0-4-0ST on the Bessemer Bank at Burnpur on 13th December 1976

BELOW A Nasmyth Wilson 2-6-0T, built at Patricroft in 1913 at Burnpur Iron and Steel Works

LEFT A triple header of classic British industrials at Kulti Ironworks on 14th December 1976. Leading is an Andrew Barclay 0-4-0ST of 1904, in the centre is an Andrew Barclay 0-6-0ST of 1919 and the train engine is a Hawthorn Leslie 0-6-0T of 1927

FAR LEFT A Mitsubishi 0-6-2T on the Coal Wharf Quay at Calcutta docks on 3rd December 1976

ABOVE A Robert Stephenson and Hawthorn 0-6-0T of 1948 draws coke from the ovens at Burnpur. The orange cloud in the background indicates that a charge of ore has just gone into the blast furnaces. 15th December 1976

LEFT An Indian Railways' HGS Class No.26721 (North British of Glasgow, 1921) draws a rake of coal wagons from Sripur Yard on 23rd December 1976

Country Boy: Indian Railways' XC
Class Pacific No.22224 in Prantik
Cutting, Bolpur, during my epic
week with this last greyhound of
British steam

Indian XC Pacifics – The Last Greyhounds of British Steam

ON MARCH 30TH 1980 the 'Sunday Times Magazine' carried pictures of the Indian XC Pacific that I had decked in LNER blue livery to emphasise the XCs' similarity to the Gresley A3s. The following week the paper received a letter from Miss Marjory Gresley, Sir Nigel's daughter, who read the story with interest but pointed out that the shade of blue was incorrect. Of course she was right, but our paint was the closest match we could get in the markets of downtown Burdwan.

By 1979 all the survivors of these former express passenger engines of the British Raj were downgraded to end their days on heavy shunting and tripping from Burdwan depot, 60 miles north of Calcutta on the main line to Delhi. During December of that year I discussed the history of these locomotives with Loco Foreman S. N. Bajpai who arranged for XC No.22226 (Vulcan Foundry 1928) to be painted in blue livery and put on the daily pick up freight to Bolpur. 'You can take Loco Inspector Anupum Banerjee and Depot Chargehand Santos Chaudhuri with you,' Bajpai said. So began one of the happiest and most memorable weeks of my life. I was living in the retiring rooms at Burdwan Station that bore a distinct resemblance to Nuneaton Trent Valley. Each morning I walked down to the depot and the XC looked magnificent standing in the yard among its begrimed sisters and WG Mikados. Our pick up freight left around 07.30 and we went main line to Khana Junction where the Bolpur line diverges.

At Bolpur I met Bhadu Das the shoeshine boy who featured in the 'Cattle Boy'. I took him to market and decked him out in blue pants and red headband to match the colour of the XC. Sitting on the bank of a Ganges tributary, he posed as a typical Bengali cattle boy as the XC smokily rolled across a beautiful stone viaduct in the background.

After an outstanding week, I left Burdwan with a heavy heart but knew that I had to return before the XCs finished. I kept in touch with Bajpai and following an urgent letter from him saying the surviving XCs would shortly be withdrawn, I returned to Calcutta at the end of February 1981 and caught the 'Black Diamond Express' to Burdwan. Bajpai and Chaudhuri met me off the train.

Only five XCs were left; I asked about the blue one and Bajpai said, 'dispatched for breaking up at Jamalpur three months ago. I have an engine set by for you'. That proved to be No.22224 (Vulcan Foundry 1929) and we agreed that she should be red. 'It will take several days to get the engine scraped down and painted, then she can go on the Bolpur pick up for a week allowing you to complete your photography,' Bajpai said. I returned to the retiring rooms and by the day watched the engine come to life. The red livery suited the XC to perfection and she looked every bit as magnificent as an LMS 'Princess Royal' but on the very day that we were due to go on line I was awoken by Bajpai with a telegram from Eastern Railway HQ in Calcutta instructing all surviving XCs to be condemned immediately and dispatched to Jamalpur under their own steam. 'WGs are coming to replace them.' Bajpai said. We called a meeting at the shed at 10.00 with Anupum Banerjee, Chaudhuri and the Divisional Manager. Dare we run No.22224 on line when officially condemned? The urgency of the telegram stemmed from the need for non-ferrous metals, especially copper fireboxes. The characteristic glint in Chaudhuri's eye brightened as he lifted a file from an adjacent cabinet, by amazing good fortune our engine was the only one with a steel firebox. This clinched the matter and we agreed to take the risk and run the engine for one week on the Bolpur pick up. We all knew the chance we were taking, if anything went wrong there could be serious repercussions from Calcutta HQ. What an incredible coincidence that the telegram had arrived on the very morning our programme was due to begin. So began another week of non-stop adventure with the team I had in 1979. Everyone got on well and all of us felt a sense of history. During this time, the withdrawn sister engines were dispatched light or in pairs to Jamalpur. One evening, returning from Bolpur, we passed No.22216 dragging No.22204. They had stopped because No.22216's tubes were leaking so badly she was preparing to return to Burdwan for attention, leaving No.22204 dumped in the station yard at Khana. On the last day of a week of remarkable photography we had arranged to have a commemorative dinner at Bajpai's house but on the run back from Bolpur we experienced delays in section and didn't reach Khana until 17.00. In order to be on time for dinner, it was decided that we should return to Burdwan by passenger train. Within minutes of getting down at Khana the Rampurhat to Burdwan express came in behind a WP Pacific. Chaudhuri joined the train while Anupum and I travelled footplate. 'Scrap iron,' Anupum snapped as he jabbed his finger towards the WP 'the XC is a superior engine in every way'. As we pulled out I moved over to the fireman's side to watch us overtake the XC.

Only one station lies on the four-track section between Khana Junction and Burdwan. I always cursed it for breaking up a potentially fast run down the main line but on this evening Tallit, as the station was called, provided a remarkable experience. As we ran in I saw that the XC had been held in the station. Our colour light flicked to green but before we departed I noticed that No.22224 had received the right of way as well.

The XC's chime whistle rang high above the WP's deeper tones as the two giants pulled out of the station side by side. It was sheer magic. Driver Sarkar was certainly going to challenge and issuing a throaty roar the XC quickly drew ahead of us. Our 11-coach express hung heavy but Anupum grabbed the WP's regulator and opened it wide while the driver advanced the cut-off. The semi-streamliner responded with a forward lurch but the XC scented the chase and, to my sheer joy, remained

ahead by several wagon lengths. The trails of smoke left by the two Pacifics as they did battle over the electrified main line was a spectacle within themselves. With maximum effort we inched our way past the XC's speeding wagons and drew alongside her. The two engines ran neck and neck, their crews exchanging shouts and waves. I was mesmerised by the sound of the XC at speed and the sight of her 6ft 2in-diameter driving wheels spinning gloriously.

What an incredible way to end the British Pacific tradition that began in 1908 when Churchward introduced his 'Great Bear' and ended that afternoon in Bengal, 73 years later, with this last greyhound of British steam. As speed increased the roar from the two engines became deafening until, after a couple of miles, the XC eased and soon disappeared in our smoke trail. When we reached Burdwan, Chaudhuri came up to the WP's footplate and explained that he had signalled Driver Sarkar to refrain from any further thrills on account of the XC's age and status.

Over dinner we discussed preservation and to allow time, Bajpai said he would put our XC at the back of the long shed and place a WG ready for a periodic overhaul in front of it, so giving the excuse of not being able to despatch the XC in the immediate future. This was done first thing the following morning.

The necessary publicity was given on my return to Britain but, predictably, the responsible authorities ignored it. The XCs became extinct and with them went a small part of me also.

PREVIOUS PAGE A line of red blossom trees between Bolpur and Bhedia form a backdrop to XC No.22224, returning to Burdwan with the Bolpur pick up on Sunday 1st March 1981. I also covered the blue XC Pacific No.22226 in Prantik Cutting. This scene makes an interesting contrast to Country Boy.

LEFT The blue XC being coaled at Burdwan before working the next morning's Bolpur pick up. As the coal is lifted a ball of fire erupts from the crane's chimney

BELOW The red XC is coaled by mobile steam crane at Burdwan prior to working the Bolpur pick up the following morning

Indian Railways' XE Class
No.22542 built by the legendary
Clydeside shipbuilder William
Beardmore of Dalmuir in 1930
seen here at Asansol, its home
depot, on 12th December 1976

The Indian XEs

I have had a passion for Indian Railways' XEs ever since I first set eyes on one at Asansol loco shed in December 1976. They were the most powerful conventional steam engines to work on the Indian sub-continent and weighed two hundred tonnes in full working order. Along with their XC Pacific relations, they epitomised the zenith of British steam development in the 1920s. Built as part of the celebrated X Series Standards, the XEs totalled 58 engines built between 1928 and 1930 for the East Indian Railway by Vulcan Foundry, Newton le Willows, Lancashire and the Clydeside shipbuilder Beardmore of Dalmuir.

The XEs spent almost half a century hauling 1,500-tonne coal trains over the hill regions of Bengal between Asansol and Jha Jha but by 1976 they were being rapidly withdrawn and dispatched to Jamalpur works for breaking up. However, by good fortune I learnt from the Eastern Railways' Chief Mechanical Engineer's office in Calcutta that at least eight XEs were to receive major overhauls at Jamalpur prior to being sold into industrial service. The details were carefully typed out for me and I resolved to cover these at a later date. The world expeditions proceeded apace and although I never forgot the XEs, I never found an opportunity to cover them.

That was until the beginning of 1989 when I realised that I had to take action. But Indian Railways' Chief Mechanical Engineer in Delhi was sceptical; 'None will exist today,' he said, 'they are an obsolete type and will have been replaced by redundant WGs by now.' They were so convinced about this that great reluctance was shown in contacting any of the locations I had listed. Equally, I was convinced that working examples could still be found. After much effort we got through to Sapura power station at Ghoradongri on the Central Railway line between Nagpur and Itarsi. They confirmed that two were there and one was working. Much encouraged we then made contact with Korba thermal power station near Bilaspur. Again the reply was positive but currently under repair. By now the CME's office was very helpful and contacted the Chunar cement factory and this contact revealed another working example and just for good

measure confirmed they had acquired a WG as a potential replacement but preferred the XE.

Two days later, on 25th January 1989, I left Delhi at 19.15 by 16 'up' Delhi to Madras in an air-conditioned two-tier sleeper and arrived at Ghoradongri at 10.00 the following morning. The small country station had the atmosphere of a long-forgotten colonial past. The station master in an immaculate white suit, greeted me; 'I am arranging a conveyance to the thermal power station,' he said. As we approached I saw two XEs in the yard and I wrote emotionally in my diary: 'they looked better than I had ever remembered, very XC-like and more Gresley than Gresley!' They were so LNER-like, it reminded me vividly of the big Pacifics I saw at Grantham as a boy. I soon learned that obtaining spare parts for the XEs was an acute problem and excess wear of bearings and steel tyres had caused the driving wheels to sheer off the rivet heads on the frame necessitating welding to restore them. I spent four magical days with the XEs at Ghoradongri before departing on the 29th January for Korba leaving by Chattisgrah Express, a night train that arrived at Bilaspur at 14.30 the following day. From here I took a bus onwards at 16.00 to reach Korba at 20.00, 23 hours after leaving Sapura.

The following morning Shri Gurcharan Singh came to the guest house and we went to his office where he introduced me to Wilfred Frank Stephens, Chief Maintenance Officer and a locomotive artisan par excellence. At the shed Wilfred presented his Y1 Class 2-8-4T ex-Great Indian Peninsular Railway. A beauty with copper firebox, D valves and Stephenson link motion, complete with inside admission and top exhaust – a superb engine in every respect.

Korba's roster included two XE/1s of 1945 ex-Western Railway; an AWE/2 that was an American war-time version of the XE; two HSM and one HS 2-8-0s. But the gem of the fleet was XE No.22502 a Beardmore engine of 1930. She was awaiting a hydraulic test and had a low chimney and low sniffing valves and of all the XEs this was the most perfect aesthetically.

The nostalgia of Korba's roster was overwhelming and I

promised Wilfred that I would return to cover No.22502 at work. No less nostalgic was the guest house garden; it was definitively English. It had a vast display of hollyhocks, pinks, blue wallflowers, Michaelmas-daisies, carnations, marigolds and roses. Through that garden my childhood past welled up and I saw my young mother tending the flowers during the post-war years. Everything was there except lupins – I looked in vain.

I left Korba by taxi on Sunday 5th February at 15.15 bound for the Chunar Cement Company. After reaching Bilaspur at 17.45 I waited until 01.15 for the express to Benares. It was two hours 45 minutes late. I remained all day on the train finally reaching Varanasi, totally exhausted, at 19.00 that evening. A night in the famous Clarke's Hotel restored my strength and the following morning I travelled the 70 kilometres to Chunar Cement. Here Mr. Pandy, the loco foreman, greeted me and I spent three happy days photographing XE No.22531 (Vulcan Foundry 1928).

The success of the XE expedition was never forgotten; as time went on I realised the historical significance of these locomotives as a missing link in the evolution of British steam and also that if any survived they would be the last big, British steam locomotives left in world service.

Exactly eight years later, in January and February 1997, I returned to India for another XE expedition visiting exactly the same locations again still with the same instinctive feeling that at least one would be found active. At Chunar, Mr. Pandy received me cordially but his XE was now out of use and the WG was active. At Ghoradongri both XEs were awaiting auction for scrap, the connecting line to Indian Railways having been electrified, but I was able to make many pictures around the theme of 'Beardmore Requiem' as both Ghoradongri's engines were from that builder. But Korba produced the ultimate triumph; XE No.22502 was working although tragically the beautiful Y1 had been broken up. I spent eight days at Korba between 28th January and 4th February and made a superb set of pictures. Diesels were on order and the XE had only weeks left in traffic.

Realising what had happened to the Y1 that was a unique period piece, I decided that something had to be done to preserve the XE. I contacted the National Railway Museum in Delhi and had meetings with the management at Korba. I wrote detailed reports for both, often sitting up on the guest house veranda until midnight. My reports revolved around five aspects:-

1) She was the last survivor of India's X Series Standards.

2) She was an example of the most powerful conventional locomotives to work on the Indian sub-continent.

3) She was the last big engine from the British school of locomotive design left in world service.

4) She was the only surviving locomotive built by the legendary Clydeside shipbuilder Beardmore of Dalmuir.

5) She was a unique example of British locomotive evolution because she was descended from Gresley's P1s of the LNER of 1925.

Immediately after I left Korba in February 1997 the XE apparently was taken out of traffic and following further meetings in Delhi, I received confirmation that No.22502 had been taken halfway across India for transfer to the National Railway Museum in Delhi. On

the following expedition in 1999 I went to the museum to see it in pride of place and took a photograph of my daughter Marie-Louise sitting on the buffer beam. It was

a fitting conclusion and I was proud to have been the catalyst in bequeathing a two-hundred-tonne monument to India's future generations.

A former Indian Railways XE class Mikado 2-8-2 at work on the Korba system during the January/February 1997 XE expedition. This superb locomotive - Indian Railways No.22502 - was the last surviving XE and was built on Scotland's Clydeside by William Beardmore of Dalmuir in 1930

This attractive Borsig (English phase) 2-8-0 was located at Deraa on the Syrian/Jordanian border. Saturday 3rd July 1976

Syria and The Pilgrims' Route to Mecca

HAVING DRIVEN OVERLAND from Britain in my motor caravan, I crossed the border between Turkey and Syria in June 1976. I knew that I would be too late for Syria's standard-gauge locos and some 40 engines – the entire Syrian fleet, including wrecks and partly dismantled engines, lay in two miserable lines at Jebrim station, 11 miles from Aleppo. The dump included Prussian G8s and G10s and some British War Department 2-10-0s.

My main interest in Syria was the Hedjaz Railway, the former pilgrim route to Mecca, and on arrival in Damascus I went to the Hedjaz station. After weeks of travel I was tired and somewhat confused, matters made worse by the sweltering heat. Within ten minutes of being there I met Hamid el How who spoke perfect English, quickly grasped the nature of my work and offered me the use of his family field in which to place my motor caravan.

He lived in the beautiful Dayarra district of Damascus, a green place in stark contrast to the dry, rocky terrain of the country at large. A vast irrigation system used pumps to lift water from an underground lake and send it via ever-changing irrigation channels to produce a vast growing area. Dayarra was famous for its plums that were second to none, several grape varieties, peaches, apples and apricots that all grew in profusion along with many appetising vegetables.

The black nights and the star-strewn sky brought a welcome coldness if not a faint chill. We would sleep out on the flat roof of Hamid's house taking full advantage of the cool relief. Figures with Arabic robes and lanterns moved throughout the plantations at night constantly changing the patterns of the water arteries against the steady, chattering rhythm of the water pumps.

Hamid proved to be a wonderful friend. He accompanied me to Cadem loco works and to the locomotive running sheds. We also enjoyed wonderful days on the line to Sergayah on the Lebanese border.

Picnic specials would run as daily excursions, especially on Fridays for the inhabitants of Damascus to obtain some relief from the searing heat of the city. They were worked by SLM-built 2-6-0Ts of the 1890s hauling vintage rakes of wooden-bodied coaches.

The pilgrims' route to Mecca was authorised by the Sultan of Turkey during the Ottoman period and was built to the curious Levantine gauge of 3ft 3⅝in. It ran south to Deraa on the Jordanian border, through Jordan and into Saudi Arabia and via Medina to Mecca. Every male Muslim was required to visit Mohammed's birthplace in Mecca at least once in his lifetime. But this was a dangerous journey in the 19th century. Turkish pilgrims were frequently attacked by Arabs hostile to Ottoman rule even though the railway was intended to carry pilgrims in safety and improved comfort.

However, marauding Arabs attacked the railway workers and in the end the line never got farther than Medina. Pilgrims had to continue on foot over the remaining 230 miles to Mecca. The railway carried pilgrims for only seven seasons until the outbreak of World War One. The Turks allied with Germany and Arab nationalists, supported by the British under Colonel Lawrence, succeeded in driving them out of the Hedjaz. To keep them out they blew up sections of the railway forcing trains to terminate at Maan in southern Jordan. Despite various proposals to re-open the line, it remains closed south of Jordan.

The Syrian section of the Hedjaz remained all steam and was worked primarily by Hartmann 2-8-0s and Mikados. At Deraa I located a Borsig 2-8-0, a beautiful engine and one of that maker's English-phase designs that pre-dated World War One.

I had an opportunity to make a footplate journey over the Hedjaz from Deraa to Damascus and back. Our locomotive was No.191, a Hartmann 2-8-0 of 1906. Departure from Deraa was heralded by a ceremonial ringing of the station bell and soon we were clattering away into the hot desert. Many tiny stations and desolate halts served small communities for whom the train would stop to order. We were restricted to a maximum speed of 34mph on account of the condition of the track although the engine rocked wildly giving an impression of a much higher speed. The locomotive had a paper speed recorder fitted. The crew were very friendly and shared cold tea with me during the journey. In one of the quiet moments when we stood at a station the driver informed me that he had two wives!

The heat of the footplate and the flames from the oil firing bursting under the firebox housing gave the impression of being in a furnace travelling through a furnace. Camouflaged military units appeared all along the way. The 75-mile journey that included 16 stops, took three hours 45 minutes. No.91's high-pitched whistle screamed continuously as we approached Damascus in the midday heat. Having uncoupled from the train we ran to the shed to prepare the locomotive for a return working three hours later.

The heat had eased slightly as we departed from Damascus at 15.00. We headed away past Cadem Works with its many derelict engines. Our train included a water wagon that was in fact an old locomotive tender, its water being dispensed to local people at stations along the way. The driver pointed to the spot where sister engine No.190 overturned after a military tank had crossed the track and put the line out of alignment. On that southbound run I watched the desert become increasingly golden in the lowering sun.

The Syrian hospitality was all pervading: 'stay the night at my station and proceed with tomorrow's train'.

On arrival at Deraa we did a few minutes' shunting before our engine retired to the shed and within half an hour it looked completely dead. Such is the rapid transformation in personality when oil-burning engines take their rest.

BELOW During my footplate journeys over the northern section of the Hedjaz with Hartmann 2-8-0 No.191 of 1906, we stopped at various locations to give passengers access to remote villages

BOTTOM LEFT After the day's intense sun, the evening's mellow

light gives relief to the border country between Syria and Lebanon. Here, a Syrian 2-6-0T leaves Sergyah on the Lebanese border and heads through the irrigated fertile highlands with a passenger train to Damascus

BOTTOM RIGHT An abandoned locomotive at Cadam Works

East Germany, Home of The World's Last Steam Expresses

DURING THE MID 1970S the world's last high-speed steam expresses were operating over the 103-mile-long racing ground between Berlin and Dresden in East Germany. Here 50-year-old Pacifics hauling trains of 500 tonnes, returned timings faster than a mile a minute and reached top speeds of 90mph fired on locally mined coal.

High-speed steam trains have always captured the imagination as epitomised by the streamlined era of the 1930s. As early as 1904, a three-figure speed was reached by the Great Western Railway's 'City of Truro' in its dash down Wellington Bank in Somerset. And even earlier, in 1892, the New York Central claimed that one of their high-stepping 4-4-0s had reached 112mph but this was not authenticated.

However, there was nothing questionable about the 'Cheltenham Flyer' that carried a headboard stating 'The World's Fastest Train' and proved it by running the 77.3 miles between Paddington and Swindon in 56 minutes 47 seconds. Scintillating as this was, it was eclipsed by the American Milwaukee Railroad's 'Hiawatha' that ran between Chicago and St Paul with Atlantics and subsequently Hudsons. Nothing has ever superseded the scintillating brilliance of the 'Hiawatha' schedule that demanded speeds of 110mph in certain sections in order to maintain time. Top-speed running was believed to be as high as 115mph.

With such a history, the East German Pacifics attracted nation-wide interest and in the summer of 1977 I drove from Britain to Germany in a motor caravan and made a number of camp bases alongside the hallowed metals of the Berlin to Dresden line. My timing proved to be perfect; not only was 1977 destined to be the last summer for steam but, had I gone a year or two earlier, problems with the police would almost certainly have been encountered. As it was, the authorities had become used to visiting foreigners photographing trains and there was little risk of being arrested.

The stars of the drama were the handsome O1 Class Pacifics, introduced in 1925 as Germany's standard express locomotives. They had a superb 1920s aura. In 1961 some were rebuilt with large boilers, smaller windshields, Boxpok driving wheels and Giesl chimneys. The rebuilds were impressive but I much preferred the stylish simplicity of the originals.

I will never forget the lovely soft countryside through which the expresses passed and the joy of camping next to the main line over so many happy days. The following random extract is taken from my diary dated June 1977: 'The rain had added clarity to the atmosphere and, as evening advanced, we heard the rhythms of the 16.48 Berlin to Bratislava as she left Grossenheim some four miles away. A lovely, hollow, reverberating sound echoed over the damp countryside. For three glorious minutes we listened to the musical roar of the O1 gently picking up speed before it reached our embankment where, well into the seventies, she whistled for Bohla station and prepared to make a fast dash down the bank into Dresden.

ABOVE The splendour of the un-rebuilt Reichsbahn 01 Pacifics is captured in this picture of the 06.37 express from Berlin to Dresden caught in the soft countryside near Grossenheim. This 50-year-old Pacific is in charge of a 450-tonne train

ABOVE Wild flowers in the East German countryside around Dresden provide an evocative foil for an un-rebuilt 01 Pacific

ABOVE LEFT The last German Mallets worked on the meter-gauge Selketalbahn in the Harz of eastern Germany. Here we see one of these turn-of-the-century 0-4-4-0Ts leaving Gernrode with an early morning train to Alexisbad in July 1977

LEFT One of the last 600mm gauge German Feldbahn 0-8-0Ts of World War One ends its days amid the Great Mullions on the Bad Muskau clay-carrying system. Wednesday 29th June 1977

Turkey

THE TURKISH EXPEDITION OF 1976 was very productive; there was still sufficient steam at work and a splendid variety of classes embracing British, French, German and American types. However, my continuous failure over several weeks to obtain any form of written permission to photograph the country's last steam locomotives despite my good connections in the country, has never failed to amaze me.

The country had several particularly fine attractions. One of these was the dense, suburban services out of Izmir on the Aegean coast.

This city that is famous for figs became equally famous for the sharp, staccato bark of steam locomotives toiling up the 1-in-37 grades away from the city, passing an incredible backdrop of suburbs with houses perched on every conceivable inch of the hillsides. Also on this system was the flat crossing at Hilal, where the lines from Izmir's Basmane station to Ciyli and Bornova crossed the lines from Izmir's Alsancak station to Buca and Sedicoy.

This intensely busy crossing produced a variety of motive power almost unimaginable today a mere 30 years later. Included were Robert Stephenson 2-8-2s of 1929; German Kreigsloks; Henschel 2-10-2s of 1932; delightfully French Humboldt 2-8-0s, built in Paris in 1912; Prussian G8, 0-8-0s and G10, 0-10-0s and some Paris-built Corpet Louvet 2-10-0s.

One keenly anticipated working at Hilal was the 09.35 mixed to Denizli. This working produced spectacular double-headed combinations such as Corpet Louvet 2-10-0s and German 2-10-2s or either of these with a Prussian G8 or G10, the possibilities being limited only by the classes found at Izmir.

Another example of Turkish delight was the isolated coal-carrying system that linked the Black Sea port of Eregli with the coal mines at Armutcuk, 11 miles along the coast. Although it is part of the Turkish State Railway, this system was isolated from the remainder of the network. It was the last haven of the Prussian G8$_2$, two-cylinder 2-8-0s. These handsome, powerful machines were a smaller version of the Prussian G12, 2-10-0s and over a thousand were built between 1927 and 1935 including 62 examples for Turkey. The coal from Armutcuk was shipped either from the docks or delivered to the huge steel complex at Eregli.

Another great attraction was the 257-mile line from Irmak to Zonguldak. This was the preserve of the massive Vulcan Iron Works 2-10-0 'Skyliners,' 88 of which were built at the Wilkes Barre works in Pennsylvania between 1947 and 1949.

The route was mountainous, scenic and heavily graded with the additional attraction of former World War Two S160, 2-8-0s on banking duties at several locations. As if this were not enough, American 'Middle East' 2-8-2s appeared on passenger trains. Such all-American drama was contrasted at Irmak by one of the Turkish Churchills, a Stanier 8F 2-8-0, one of 20 sent to Turkey in 1942.

Izmir's resident turkeys find the presence of Turkish Railways' Baldwin 'Middle East' 2-8-2 No.46204 somewhat intimidating

Turkish State Railways operated
several ex-Prussian designs
including G82s. Two are seen
here working at Eregli

TOP Turkish State Railways'
No.56517 crosses the viaduct at
Egridir on Thursday 25th June
1987

ABOVE A brace of American-built
Turkish 'Skyliner' 2-10-0s boil up
at Irmak

LEFT A Prussian G8 0-8-0
No.44071 peeps out of the small
longhouse at Burdur while being
prepared for duty

Karabuk Iron and Steel Works, Turkey

ULKU STEELWORKS AT KARABUK is located on the line from Irmak to Zonguldak on the Black Sea coast. This line was the haunt of the American-built 'Skyliner' 2-10-0s.

Kemel Ataturk, the Turkish hero, was instrumental in planning the works and his death in 1938 coincided with its opening. It was the country's first steel works and its remote location, in an amphitheatre of hills, was chosen as security against air attacks. Abundant coal came from collieries along the Black Sea coast while the iron ore that could be up to 70 per cent iron content, came from Sivas far away to the east. Steel production at Ulku at the time of my visit in 1976, was 750,000 tonnes a year.

The works were very dramatic and the structures highly animated. Plumes of steam issued from the coking plant, orange smoke drifted across the works each time a charge of iron ore went into the blast furnaces; steam and smoke issued from a dozen points, and flange piping, like an endless snake, embraced many structures. High above the turmoil a bleeder pipe spouted a tongue of flame.

Tantalising views of British locomotives could be seen moving through the structures including Hawthorn Leslie-designed 0-6-0STs and a pair of Bagnall 0-8-0Ts, delivered in 1938 for the works opening.

Gaining entry was difficult, as it was to most railway locations in Turkey at that time. In Ankara I had received the friendship and support of the son of a government minister. I had stayed at his house, attended the Turkish Senate and regularly walked the corridors of power but no one could produce a letter of authority that would permit me to photograph steam trains!

From the hotel on my first night I experienced a remarkable phenomenon, the whole town suddenly became illuminated in a vivid orange glow that even lit the hills beyond the town.

Having reached a climax, the glow quickly faded and, like a black shadow, darkness closed in again. I was mystified, no charge to the blast furnace or coke ovens would produce such a cataclysmic effect.

Next morning I explored the area behind the blast furnaces where huge piles of iron ore lay. An S160, 2-8-0 shunted the connection with the state railway. There were also enormous piles of scrap metal containing pieces of locomotives cut up at Sivas works including Reichbahn three-cylinder 2-10-0s along with older Mogul and various tank classes.

Later that day I discovered the slag bank. I had never seen one before and was captivated by the sight of Hawthorn Leslie 0-6-0STs bringing ladles of molten waste from the furnaces out to the periphery of the complex and emptying them down the slag bank. I remember wondering if this operation at Ulku was unique in using steam power.

Then it dawned on me. Those ghastly glows the night before had been created by the periodic tipping of molten slag. I was able to make a range of pictures of the entire operation, both by day, with sunlight and cloud-flecked skies, at twilight and, of course, by night.

One of Karabuk's Newcastle-built
0-6-0STs from Robert Stephenson
and Hawthorne empties a
cauldron of molten slag during
August 1976

ABOVE Karabuk had two heavy-duty Bagnall Side Tanks of 1937, one is seen here emptying molten slag during the night shift

RIGHT One of Karabuk Steel Works' Bagnall 0-8-0Ts of 1937 waits patiently for the ladles to fill with molten steel

BELOW RIGHT Karabuk's Hawthorn Leslie 0-6-0ST No.3302, built in 1937, empties molten waste down the bank on Wednesday 11th August 1976

Pot Girls, India

THE VARIOUS POT GIRLS THAT have appeared in my pictures over the years may seem fanciful but they are merely a formalised arrangement of an everyday scene, particularly in India's villages and country areas. The Pot Girls are an extension of the Cattle Boy and Country Boy themes made at Bolpur in 1979 and 1981 respectively. Cattle Boy is perhaps the best picture I have ever made, it is certainly the one I have always tried to better with the various pot girls. I thought I had achieved this at Korba in February 1987 on the XE expedition. The girl's posture, clothes and serene gaze were a captivating foil to the AWE Mikado smokily crossing the river bridge in the background. The AWEs were an Americanised version of the British XE Mikado and came in stark contrast to them. The original British XE would have looked better.

Another close contender had been done at Khatauli Sugar Mill in February 1981 when a girl with a pitcher at her side, provided a tranquil foil to the passing of a 600mm-gauge Baldwin 4-6-0T from World War One. This is a very moving picture. The positions of the girl and the train make a perfect relationship and the stately pillars of what is otherwise a very ordinary little bridge, give a classical feeling that the girl more than lives up to.

But if Cattle Boy has ever been beaten, and I don't think he has, it would be with the work I did on the Wankaner to Morvi line in Gujarat with Gaytriba Rana who was 13. It was February 1999, a particularly emotionally charged time, as this was the last steam-worked line in India and I worked with her over five days.

She knew not a word of English but she enjoyed the shoots and was both placid and patient. We developed a terrific working relationship, she was not camera sensitive and several of the takes during that unforgettable week have a great presence. The pictures with her make a memorable tribute to the end of steam in India.

Gaytriba Rana with the afternoon passenger train from Morvi to Wankaner headed by a metre-gauge YG Class 2-8-2 Mikado

ABOVE LEFT This scene was made during the 'Cattle Boy' session at Bolpur in December 1979 and features Indian Railways' XE No.22226 in blue livery

FAR LEFT One of several 'Pot Girl' sessions at Korba with ex India Railway's XE class 2-8-2 No22502 built by William Beadmore's clydeside shipyard in 1930. The XEs consisted of a class of 58 locomotives delivered to the east Indian Railway between 1928/30

LEFT A theme on the Nidadavolu to Bhimavaran line in Andhra Pradesh featuring Indian Railways' WT Class 2-8-4T No.14011 that was allocated to Rhajamundry for working cross-country trains around the Godavri Delta

Down at the Local Ironworks, Brazil

ALTHOUGH SAO PAULO was the fastest-growing and most populous city in the world at the time of my visit in 1978, it was also a city with a soul despite its many social problems. The city had long since abandoned any vestiges of its torpid past, now it was a place where entrepreneurialism could flourish and fortunes could be made among its skyscrapers and green parks. Its cultural life was rich and embraced all nationalities making it the most modern, multi-racial city on Earth. Sao Paulo Museum of Art on Avenue Paulista was a veritable treasure house.

Sao Paulo was a superb staging point for a number of famous steam locations like the unique cable-operated railway up the Serra do Mar with its Kerr Stewart brake engines, the national wagon works at Cruzeiro with its Shrewsbury-built Sentinels, the Perus-Pirapora cement railway and the Cosim Ironworks at Mogi das Cruzes.

Cosim Ironworks was located next to the main line from Sao Paulo to Rio de Janeiro. I caught a suburban train from Sao Paulo Luz station and on approaching the works, saw the almost unbelievably huge chimney of one of the Baldwin 0-6-2STs as it ran through the structures.

The works had two of these 5ft 6in-gauge Baldwins that were delivered to the Paulista Railway in 1896 and were pensioned off to the ironworks in 1944. These classic American switchers made the ultimate contrast at Cosim to a pair of Sharp, Stewart 0-4-0STs built in Glasgow in 1898 and 1903 respectively. These were ex-Sao Paulo Railway. They were Scottish 'Pugs' although the 1903 engine had an hybridised smokebox and an extended bunker while its sister engine had a stove-pipe chimney that evoked memories of Glasgow's Springburn and could not have been more different than the enormous stack on the Baldwins.

One unfortunate incident occurred during an otherwise magnificent day in Cosim when I took the 1903 Sharp, Stewart down a disused line to make a rural picture. As the engine inched its way along the rusty overgrown metals we struck the branch of a tree that damaged the engine's whistle causing a large jet of steam to shoot skywards and necessitating the fire to be dropped.

My visit was on Monday 20th November 1978 and the following is an extract from my diary for that day: 'The five furnaces each discharged their molten steel into huge cauldrons every few hours. These are then lifted by overhead cranes before the molten steel is transferred into moulds to form ingots. The locomotives then take these to the rolling mill and the sight of the archaic 0-6-2STs conveying a load of ingots against a fiery backdrop of molten steel was exotic. The engines issued continuous clouds of coal smoke and with rasps from incorrect valve settings they dropped flaming cinders along the track while their whistles blared like angry banshees against the all-enveloping clamour and tremor of the works'.

ABOVE AND TOP LEFT One of the Cosim Baldwin 0-6-2STs in scenes that emphasize the 5ft 6in-gauge and enormous chimney of this typical American Switcher

RIGHT Builder's plate of the Sharp, Stewart 0-4-0ST

LEFT Cosim's Sharp, Stewart 0-4-0ST makes a superb contrast with its American counterparts

The Maria Fumacas of Campos State, Brazil

ONE OF BRAZIL'S GREATEST steam attractions was its sugar fields and in particular those of Campos State. I was excited to visit these for their preponderance of American locomotives, having missed documenting America's indigenous steam. The journey from Rio de Janeiro to Campos revealed a landscape of much beauty. Many of the green hills had completely bald tops except for the odd clump of trees that appeared to grow out of the stone. The invariably cloudy sky was washed with myriad shades of luminous grey and periodically radiant sunlight would burst through, often in the distance, causing isolated strips of landscape far away to illuminate. The exotic flowering trees and red soil presented vivid colours. As we travelled our movement caused one particular red flowering tree to move its position from a succession of green backgrounds until it rotated in front of a bright texture of orange soil. At that moment, illuminated by a sudden shaft of sunlight, the combination exploded into an orgasm of colour.

When we reached Campos I went to the outeiro usina (sugar mill) where I was greeted by the owner Dr. Inojosa and his wife Dona Angela. The most comfortable accommodation had been provided and I was able to enjoy photographing their all-American roster that consisted of an 0-4-0, two Moguls, two Consolidations and one Mikado.

I had some wonderful adventures with Outeiro's No.7, a Baldwin-built 2-8-0 with a wooden cab. This engine had the capacity to emit constant clouds of black smoke. My first trip was on the line to Murundum but constant derailments caused by the previous day's heavy rains prevented us from getting there. On one occasion all No.7's wheels came off the track and embedded themselves in mud. This took an hour and a half to correct. A track trolley followed us in an attempt to make good the rain-inflicted damage. Unusually, No.7 had two flangeless driving wheels to enable tight curves to be traversed and this caused the flanges on the other wheels to squeal loudly. Although we were far out in the canefields, we never lost sight of Outeiro's three smoking chimneys that were visible against the mountains and

washed in a blue haze. We collected loaded wagons from several sidings but because of the delays, our return journey was by moonlight. We had a long rake of loaded cane cars and No.7's black exhaust fanned out for half a mile behind us in the damp, evening air. On a horseshoe curve, where our last wagon was parallel to the engine, the smoke trail echoed the curvature perfectly. The journey was further enhanced by the millions of fireflies glittering with twisting and turning movements over the adjacent fields.

The Brazilians call their steam locomotives 'Maria Fumacas' or 'Smoke Marys'.

I had many adventures at other usinas in the Campos area using Outeiro as my base. These visits were well constituted because Dr. Inojosa was president of the Copper Flue Co-operative and most other mills were members. One morning we took the Copper Flue van from Outeiro to Macabu Usina and on the road from Campos saw a beautiful 19th century 4-4-0 running backwards with a string of cane cars. The train swept over a crossing in front of us and the engine's whistle had a deep Stanier-like tone and the bell, mounted on top of the boiler, rang continuously. She was obviously a former main-line passenger engine.

That magnificent locomotive became top priority and I traced it to Sao Jose Usina. It proved to be a Sharp, Stewart built in Glasgow in 1892 for Brazil's Mogiana Railway. The engine left main-line service for the Santa Cruz Usina and around 1948 she was traded in exchange for air pumps and other mill equipment and so arrived at Sao Jose. An identical sister engine was cut up at Sao Jose in the early 1970s but this engine's red number plate still lay in the stores.

I was able to do some wonderful pictures of the Sharp, Stewart in the canefields at night and once waited for the engine at a remote loading siding. The clear sky showed many constellations, including a lovely view of the Milky Way. A new moon rose and bats, owls, frogs and moths came out in profusion. Fireflies also abounded and I even had the pleasure of catching one. The clear night was enhanced by distant canefield blazes. Following the harvest the stubble was burnt off to fertilise the soil and not infrequently these fires were started by errant sparks from the locomotives. It was well into the evening before the 86 year old arrived. I was thrilled to see this ghost of Springburn drifting through the tropical Brazilian night.

After photography I stowed my equipment in the engine's tender and rode back on the footplate. The journey back included a stretch on the mainline network and we had to wait for the overnight train from Rio to go by. The Sharp, Stewart was a superb engine to ride, especially on the excellently maintained national railway. Fire swirled around the engine's chimney as we headed our long rake of cane through total darkness. There was no electric lights for many miles.

It was the end of a long day and the heat of the tropical night, combined with that of the firebox, caused the driver to fall asleep at the regulator but the fireman fought drowsiness and maintained the boiler pressure at 150psi, although to achieve this meant continuously throwing logs into the firebox. It was nearly midnight before we arrived back at the yard at Sao Jose.

In Usina Santa Maria I became very attached to another extraordinary engine. It was ex-Leopoldina Railway No.204, one of a batch of Moguls that had been built by Beyer Peacock of Manchester in 1899. This wood burner, decked in green livery, had a rusty stove pipe chimney that had been eaten away around the rim by fire over the years.

This mill had other delightful engines, including a huge 1943-built American Mikado with a whippoorwill whistle that could be heard for miles around and an elegant North British-built 2-8-0 of 1904. The operations manager was Senor Ary and he had been requested to help me with my programme of photography.

Looking back, I realise that I was somewhat over zealous in my requests: move engines, steam them, have them cleaned, stop them, start them or reverse them. Requests that, when combined with the daily operational problems of running the network, proved an ever-increasing strain for Senor Ary. As the days slipped by he became ever less in evidence and by the end of my visit, he could not be found at all.

I suppose I have always been prepared to die for my art and have mistakenly believed that others are prepared to do the same. If Senor Ary ever reads these words I hope he can take some comfort from the wonderful pictures made at Santa Maria.

ABOVE The engine's original Beyer Peacock chimney has been eaten away as a result of constant fiery endeavours

LEFT Builder's plate detail with running number

LEFT This delightful 4-6-0 was built in 1906 by Robert Stephenson of Newcastle upon Tyne for Brazil's meter-gauge Leopoldina Railway. Long since pensioned off into industrial service, she is caught here heading through blazing canefields at the Conceicao de Macabu Usina on Thursday 31st October 1978

BELOW Oiling the driving wheels of Conceicao de Macabu Usina's Robert Stephenson 4-6-0. This former passenger-hauling locomotive has large diameter driving wheels as did San Jose's Sharp, Stewart 4-4-0

LEFT Sao Jose Usina's immaculate Sharp, Stewart 4-4-0 of 1892

The Teresa Cristina Railway, Brazil

THE TERESA CRISTINA was one of the world's finest steam railways and I was privileged to spend almost four weeks on the system in November and December 1978. Located in south-eastern Brazil, the system was 100-per-cent steam operated and carried low-grade coal from the Serra do Mar mines to the Atlantic port at Imbituba. The railway's headquarters were based in the town of Tuberao.

The Teresa Cristina was famous for its classic American steam power scaled down to meter-gauge operation. Its roster included the world's last Texas type 2-10-4s that came from Baldwin's and ALCO's works in 1940. These engines were previously on the Central Railway of Brazil. The Texas types were supported by Mikado 2-8-2s along with three simple 2-6-6-2 Mallets built by Baldwin in 1950 for working the curvaceous Lauro Muller line.

The loco shed at Tuberao was full of smoky intrigue with giant engines coming and going and clanking their way through the soot-laden gloom and the dripping water columns. A sooty pall, visible for miles around, hung high in the air above the depot.

I was fortunate to establish from the outset a great friendship with Antonio Costa Netto, one of the railway's operators. Costa spoke not a word of English nor I a word of Portuguese but we communicated superbly and I marvelled that the understanding between us was better than it might have been with many people who spoke English. He took a keen interest in my work and provided essential information on train movements each day, so enabling the best to be got from the long stints on the lineside. Apart from the pictures, this enabled me to experience the Texas 2-10-4s highballing along with 2,000-tonne trains at speeds up to 60mph.

The lineside days were unforgettable. I would rise at 04.00 and leave the depot on the footplate of the locomotive that formed the 05.00 departure with empties. We would head out for the mines and the train would stop specially to drop me off at the chosen photographic location. Each morning there would be a succession of empty wagon trains heading back to the mine. My favourite location was around marshland at KM59 with Tuberao just visible on the horizon. Unfortunately the clouds of mosquitoes did not subside until 07.00. Here I was able to photograph a particularly colourful Water Rail between trains and I enjoyed seeing this secretive bird on a number of successive days.

The lineside work was not easy and although some of my best work was done on the Teresa Cristina, heat, humidity, tiredness and mosquitoes all took their toll.

One way I did assuage the heat was to work around Sideropolis Tunnel where crystal-clear water cascaded down the rocks alongside the tunnel entrance. Here one could strip off completely and bath in the cool water. This cool, green place was protected by the tunnel on one side and a high vertical rock embankment on the other.

While on the Teresa Cristina I had the pleasure of meeting the celebrated, globe-trotting American photographer Ron Ziel. He was Mr America, complete with big hat, big intellect, big voice and big heart. He was a wonderful companion and we enthused over railway matters worldwide, not least the endless delights of the Teresa Cristina. Costa found Ron Ziel fascinating and did some hilarious impersonations of him. Costa was particularly fascinated by Ron firing off flash guns in the depot yard at night and his best imitation was excitedly running around the veranda at his house throwing lit matches into the air to represent the flashes while imitating Ron's commanding voice.

Many happy evenings were spent at Costa's house that overlooked the depot. We sat listening to the engines as they returned to the shed at all hours up to midnight. An indication of how involved Costa was with his work can be judged by his knowledge of each locomotive, the system had 14 Texas type 2-10-4s and he knew each one by its exhaust beat.

It was on the Teresa Cristina that 'Sunday Stoker', one of my best-known pictures, was done. One afternoon I went down to the depot when the sun was shining through the shrouds of smoke and steam rising from engines that appeared as black silhouettes. Fortunately Costa was with me and I asked him to get lights put on

137

two of the engines. No sooner had he done this than a steam raiser walked across the picture carrying his shovel. And so was made 'The Sunday Stoker', a picture devoted to the quietness on a Sunday when the sheds were full of locomotives breathless for the new week's working and kept alive by the steam raisers who flit from engine to engine to tend the fires and keep the boilers topped up with water.

My weeks on the Teresa Cristina were some of the happiest and most productive of all my world tours, notwithstanding a dental operation in Tuberao following a period of excruciating pain.

This short-haul freight on the Teresa Cristina Railway has a Baldwin 2-8-2 of 1946 in charge known as 'Grimy Hog'. Originally she worked on Brazil's Centro Oeste network. 'Hog' is a typical American product, scaled down to meter-gauge operation

LEFT A scene at the running shed of the Teresa Cristina Railway in Tuberao

BELOW Steam raisers flitted from engine to engine to tend fires and keep boilers topped up with water. Steam locomotives have to be kept hot and ready and maintained in light steam during days of rest. This is more economical than dropping the fire completely. So came together the ingredients for one of my best-known pictures, 'The Sunday Stoker'. 11th December 1978

Presidente Carlos Antonio Lopez, Paraguay

IT WAS CHRISTMAS EVE 1978 when I arrived in Asuncion the capital of Paraguay, having travelled overland from Brazil. A Christmas present awaited me as four vintage locomotives simmered majestically in the ancient depot. Paraguay's great attraction was the all-steam main line that ran from Asuncion to the Argentinian border at Encarnacion, so providing through services to Buenos Aires. The 230-mile line had deteriorated badly since it was converted to standard gauge by Edwardian engineers.

On Christmas Day I left Asuncion for Sapucai where the railway works were situated. The train had nine bogie coaches decked in brown livery and included a restaurant car and first-class accommodation. But the system was desperately the worse for wear. The trains had no brakes and the track was appalling, it was held together by soil and weeds and rotten sleepers confined our speed to a crawl. The railway had been under British ownership until 1961 when it was nationalised. In celebration, the new administration had applied 'Republica del Paraguay' emblems to the engines' smokebox doors. All the locomotives were woodburners and the system remained completely steam worked.

Sapucai is a tiny village some 50 miles from Asuncion. Few roads serve the area and the village streets are grassy avenues lined with flowering trees. It would be difficult to find a more incongruous setting for a railway works. The scene inside belonged to the 19th century. All the machinery, including drills and lathes, was driven by steam generated by boilers taken from withdrawn locomotives. A charcoal furnace was used for smelting and alongside stood a pair of huge steam hammers built in Yorkshire by Thwaites Bros. of Bradford. In complete contrast, the works hooter was in the very finest of Lancastrian traditions.

My accommodation in Sapucai was spartan; a room with bare walls and a camp bed on a dirt floor. With no guide, communication was extremely difficult and the villagers were quite indifferent to my presence. Sapucai had its own timeless rhythms, the village took a siesta during the lazy heat haze of the afternoons and at 17.00, when the works closed and the industry fell silent, a chorus of tree bugs took over.

The evenings in Sapucai were magical. Black velvet nights, free from the reflected wash of electricity, highlighted constellations with a resilience unknown and unimaginable to western, urban society. My boarding house was immediately next to the railway and I would sit outside in the balmy night air with a cigar and a glass of whisky watching the Edwardian Moguls expel shrouds of fire high into the sky, a situation that put me as close to paradise as I might reasonably expect to get. Throughout the night the lowing of cattle mixed with the sounds of the slide-valve engines engaged in heavy shunting, made a blissful symphony laced with the

crowing cock long before the break of dawn. The scourge of this paradise were the mosquitoes. Before sleeping, I had to cover myself with repellent and after a hot night, I would awake feeling horribly sticky necessitating a head-to-toe wash at the icy cold well in the backyard. Day break revealed a clear, dew-speckled earth. Chickens ranged freely around the homesteads while the cows came in for milking. In such places as Sapucai, one can think in light vein of multi-storey developments, traffic jams, inflation, the rapid pace of living and all the attendant neuroses of the west.

Asuncion to Encarnacion takes 18 hours, an average speed of 13mph. From Sapucai I journeyed the remaining length of the line to Encarnacion. My engine was Mogul No.103, built by the North British of Glasgow in 1910.

The tranquil landscape trickled slowly past the coach windows and wafts of sweet-smelling wood smoke drifted through the train. Refuelling was done intermittently from log piles in lineside villages. We passed through beautiful forests, many ravaged by fires caused by the Moguls. Dense woods stood precariously alongside whole areas of blackened ash. Trees had been reduced to grotesque stumps that stood alongside the cindered remains of lineside fences. Contorted strands of barbed wire noosed the burnt remains of posts and creaked eerily in the breeze. Even some of the wooden sleepers had been reduced to ashes. The farmers had long since learned to plant their prized crops at least a half a mile away from the main line. Locals populated the landscape wearing huge sombreros as protection against the searing heat.

On one occasion the train stopped on a bridge over a culvert and the engine sucked water through a pipe lowered into the trickling, muddy stream. It took an hour to fill the tender during which time No.103 hissed and slurped vigorously.

Encarnacion depot resembled an Irish shed scene from the 1920s with two Edwardian 2-6-2Ts in sleepy repose. They were built in Newcastle upon Tyne by Hawthorn Leslie between 1910 and 1913. These engines worked the short branch to the port of Pacucua. From here a wood-fired paddle steamer took the rolling stock across the Rio Parana to the Argentinian side where it continued its journey over the Urquiza Railway to Buenos Aires.

FAR LEFT A mixed-freight heads away from San Salvador

ABOVE 'Encarnacion,' a Mogul built in 1953 by the Yorkshire Engine Company's Meadowhall Works in Sheffield

The World's Last Steam Tram, Paraguay

THE WORLD'S LAST STEAM TRAM was one of the most exciting priorities of my Latin-American expedition. It was working in Paraguay at the Tebicuary Sugar Factory that was located on the international all-steam main line running from Asuncion, the Paraguayan capital, to Encarnacion on the Argentinian border. My journey to Tebicuary was from San Salvador and I rode footplate on Yorkshire Engine Company Mogul No.152 'Asuncion'. This engine, with its distinct L.M.S. aura, was built at the Meadowhall Works in 1953 for the Central del Paraguay Railway.

We left San Salvador at 06.10, just after a flaming red sun-rise had introduced the new day. The wood burner made a laboured start with a long rake of wagons. The track was largely weeded over and in places cows could be seen grazing on the alignment. The third man on the engine spent much of his time throwing logs into the tender from the leading wagon of the train that acted as an auxiliary tender. This was dangerous, back-breaking work, some logs overshot their mark and rolled down into the cab and others missed completely and disappeared over the side of the tender. When the engine was working hard its voracious consumption of wood was remarkable.

On adverse grades 'Asuncion' slipped to walking pace and the third man would transfer from the auxiliary wagon to the front of the locomotive and spray the tracks with sand. Our train was a pick up freight and we stopped at sleepy wayside stations with small sidings invariably populated by chickens and pigs. The beautiful villages had streets of grass and were delightfully untouched by roads.

On arrival at Tebicuary I was greeted with the sight of the tram engine in the factory yard. She was one of two standard-gauge examples built by Borsig of Berlin in 1910. For many years these engines worked in the streets of Buenos Aires before being pensioned off to the sugar fields of neighbouring Paraguay for a further lease of active life.

Tebicuary had a network of meter-gauge lines with a stud of German engines that included 0-4-0WT, 0-8-0 and 2-8-2s, all festooned with amazing smoke stacks.

These engines brought the cane in from the surrounding plantations. The sacks of processed sugar were then taken on the standard-gauge metals by the tram to connect with the main-line railway. During shunting movements the tram actually ran along a section of the international main line.

Photographing so many fascinating engines in the peace and tranquillity of Tebicuary was delightful. At night, the pension where I was staying reverberated with a deafening chorus of tree bugs while the biggest giant toads I have ever seen came out to enjoy the relative cool of the evening.

The tram engine was a fascinating variation on the conventional steam locomotive. They proliferated on road-side tramways and found particular favour in Holland and subsequently in the Dutch East Indies. Most of the last survivors were concentrated in Java working on rural tramways that in some cases involved on-street running.

A steam tram on the main line. During its shunting movements the steam tram at Tebicuary often ran onto the international, all-steam, main line that connected Asuncion, the Paraguayan capital, with Encarnacion on the Argentinian border

143

Fire Throwers of The Paraguayan Chacao

DEEP IN THE FORESTS of the Paraguayan Chacao grows the mighty quebracho tree that was the world's only source of tannin for the processing of leather. A network of railways developed on the Chacao to convey the trunks to the river Paraguay prior to their journey by river to Buenos Aires for export.

The last of these railway systems was based at Peurto Casado that was so remote it required a flight on a Paraguayan Airforce six-seater Cessna from the capital Asuncion to get there. It was a flight I will never forget. As we approached the runway, the plane sounded more like a lorry grinding its way up a hill. For the first time I wondered if a collection of old locomotives were worth the agony but once we were airborne and heading north the exhilaration of flying in such a plane became evident.

We followed the mighty Paraguay river that like a gleaming silver sword, cuts through a landscape of myriad tones of green. Occasionally I could pick out the route of former quebracho lines radiating from the river. As we landed on the airstrip in Peurto Casado mud shot across the windows, the result of heavy rain, and the humidity struck like being immersed in a warm damp sheet.

There were no roads leading to Peurto Casado and the town possessed only three motor vehicles. The guest house was a wooden building surrounded by dense forest. There was concern about a tarantula that had been seen there that afternoon, while just in front of the veranda, humming birds extracted nectar from flowering trees. The air was alive with insects and the sounds from the forest were strange and diverse. Here was the glory of creation as I had never experienced it before.

Before 1899 the quebracho logs were shipped to Europe for processing but subsequently this work was carried out at Peurto Casado and this was heightened by the first engine I saw in the form of 'Laurita', a 76cm-gauge 0-4-0WT built by Artur Koppel of Berlin in 1898 and bearing a plate that stated 'Primera Locomotora del Chacao Paraguayo'. Another favourite engine was No.5 'Don Carlos', a 2-8-2WT built by Manning Wardle of Leeds in 1916 but running as an 0-8-2. This engine had a

Midland Railway-type whistle that was the clearest and loudest I had ever heard. It also had a glorious rhythm comprised of one long beat followed by three rapid ones. Complete with its superb brass dome, 'Don Carlos' was an engine of great character.

One morning I rode out on one of the lines with 'Don Carlos' and on the walk from the guest house to the railway yard, I saw a huge supply boat arrive carrying passengers and supplies. The lovely old vessel silhouetted against the early morning light looked like a romantic scene from the Mississippi.

On the journey with 'Don Carlos', we passed many quebracho trees with their exotic red flowers. The wild life was breathtaking; eagles, screaming parrots, herons, butterflies, moths and grasshoppers were everywhere and the pure air was full of flying insects. Chacao Indians also were to be seen along the journey.

Photography was made very difficult by the heat and the humidity, it was more than 42 degrees centigrade. Every movement, every thought, had to be directed towards saving energy. A midday rest was essential or debilitation would set in followed by complete exhaustion.

On our return journey with a rake of quebracho logs, 'Don Carlos' began a spectacular fire display in the gathering gloom. No train ever needed a whistle at night on the Paraguayan Chacao because shrouds of crimson embers shoot a hundred feet into the air from the locomotives and trains can be seen approaching from far away. The fire throwers of the Paraguayan Chacao represent a whole new dimension in the appreciation of steam trains.

I love the Chacao; the little shops along the waterfront sold warm bread and cheese soufflés and Matte tea was drunk continuously. In the evenings many people would bathe in the river as the sun turned the water into liquid gold and the arrival of an evening Cessna plane looked no bigger than the vultures that inhabited the port.

Tranquillity was only momentarily interrupted by the wail of a steam locomotive or the clatter of a steam crane seen in silhouette against the piles of quebracho logs.

ABOVE The beautiful brass-domed
Manning Wardle 'Don Carlos' in
fiery mood at Puerto Casado

RIGHT 'Laurita', Peurto Casado's
No.1, heads a train loaded with
quebracho logs into Puerto Casado

ABOVE A scene at kilometre post 27 on the Puerto Casado system. The crew take their midday break in the wild Chacao scrublands while 'Don Carlos', a 2-8-2WT built by Manning Wardle of Leeds in 1916, simmers patiently in the background

ABOVE 'Laurita', Peurto Casado's No.1, trundles through the wild Chacao scrublands at the head of a train of quebracho logs bound for the river Paraguay at Peurto Casado

LEFT Quayside steam crane at Peurto Casado

Santa Fe, Argentina

AT SANTA FE, on Argentina's meter-gauge Belgrano Railway, I found a former Santa Fe Railway 10A-Class Prairie built in Switzerland in 1911 by Societe Suisse. The design was particularly distinctive when seen in side profile and the oxidised white boiler, complete with rusty stove-pipe chimney, provided a superb basis for photography.

Nevertheless something was missing, a strong colour had to be introduced, so I obtained a tin of red paint and applied it to the motion and running plate that both normally would have been red anyway. The result looked very powerful but one problem remained, the background was awful. A painter can easily tone down incongruous elements, a photographer often cannot. The answer was to obliterate the background with smoke. Fortunately, although originally a wood burner, the engine had been converted to burn oil. The density of its exhaust not only obliterated the background but the intense blackness of the smoke flared up the other colours and made a dramatic portrayal of an unusual locomotive. However, there were complaints to the depot from local residents about the level of pollution.

About 20 years after that experience at Santa Fe my company, Milepost 92½, was given custody of the photographic legacy of the Rev A. W. V. Mace by his widow Helen. She later became godmother to Antaeus and Dominion, my twin boys. I wrote two books on Arthur Mace's photography one of which was published by Milepost and, as an appreciation, Helen bought a gift that she said would please us.

A heavy box duly arrived and inside was a weather vane in the form of a locomotive. Not just any locomotive, but one taken from my picture of the 10A at Santa Fe with exactly the same side-profile contours. Helen had no knowledge of this connection when she ordered it.

Interested that a weather-vane manufacturer had used one of my pictures in this way I telephoned them. They flatly denied that they had copied anything and pretended that the representation was entirely the product of imagination. Obviously they thought I was after a royalty but nothing was further from my mind. Our weathervane was duly bolted onto the masonry of the high chimney at Milepost where it remains and since then I have seen others around the country.

The story constitutes a remarkable chain of events but that is not all. Several years after the Milepost weathervane was put into place a strange phenomenon occurred. The chimney of the engine on our weathervane had become covered in a dark orange rust – exactly the same tone as its ancestor in Santa Fe.

ABOVE A scene at Santa Fe on Argentina's meter-gauge Belgrano Railway with Societe Suisse 2-6-2 No.4606 obliterating an incongruous background with clouds of black oil smoke. Tuesday 20th March 1979

LEFT Later that day, No.4606 departed from Santa Fe with a short goods train

British Steam on The Pampas, Argentina

IN HIS FOREWORD to Doug Purdom's book 'British Steam on the Pampas', Andrew Henderson wrote: 'In this world of change, much information of historical value and interest in specific fields is liable to be lost or destroyed due to lack of interest and carelessness'.

In February 1948, the British-owned railways of Argentina were handed over to the Argentinian government. The seven railways concerned constituted the largest British commercial enterprise ever to operate outside the mother country. The impact of these British-owned railways on life and activity in Argentina was profound. For a hundred years the British- owned railways of Argentina had provided incalculable benefit for both countries. It was one of the greatest achievements in British industrial history. The largest of the seven railways was the Buenos Aires and Great Southern (BAGS). In its 1926 advertising it claimed to be the greatest transport enterprise in the southern hemisphere. In the 1920s, Britain's railways in the Argentine reached a peak of splendour that has seldom been bettered anywhere else in the world.

The magnificence of Argentina's railways continued for another two decades following the government take-over, before a rapid decline set in that was accelerated, as ever, by road interests.

By the time of my visit in 1978 it could be said that the railway had died with steam. The state of the track, the rolling stock and the infrastructure was appalling and deeply distressing to anyone who has any semblance of an idea about the role railways should play in society.

Approximately 2,700 locomotives are said to have been exported by British builders to Argentina and almost all of them were of typical British styling. The historical importance and the elegance of these designs were some of the major attractions that prompted my six-month expedition to Latin America.

In Buenos Aires I was fortunate to be able to stay with Richard Campbell and his wife Marcela in the former house of Doug Purdom, the last Chief Mechanical Engineer of the BAGS. My guide in Argentina was Hector Cusinato who had a burly bodyguard kind of figure, a square jaw and a double-breasted jacket under which, I always fantasised, a hand gun was concealed.

Hector's demeanour was like something out of 'The Godfather'. Although he spoke no English he was a wonderful travelling companion and communication was seldom a problem.

Buenos Aires Constitucion Station was a magnificent Victorian edifice that inside resembled London's Waterloo station in many ways. Sadly, the brilliant three-cylinder 8E Class 2-6-4Ts no longer handled the suburban traffic and the former BAGS works at Escalada no longer overhauled steam.

Steam did remain active in various depots around the system and we caught the El Atlantico Express to the coastal city of Mar del Plata. The journey through flat green pampas revealed many coots, plovers, egrets and gulls. Along the route we passed disused sheds with broken water columns and derelict sidings. Maipu shed possessed two British engines that were peeping out of the shed with derelict stares. The permanent way was in such bad condition that periodically we were physically lifted out of our seats as the coach reared up alarmingly.

Mar del Plata was a seaside resort built up by the railway. It had a pier and was very reminiscent of Bournemouth. At the loco shed we met Richard Woodward, an ex-patriot born in Liverpool in 1893 who had left for the Argentine in 1907. At 85 he still had his Lancashire accent, he spoke like George Formby and looked like Lowry! One could feel the magnificence of the BAGS in every word he spoke. He had controlled the BAGS' interests at the port of Bhia Blanca.

One of the most important classes on my itinerary was the Edwardian 12A Class 4-6-0, built as two-cylinder compounds with 6ft-diameter driving wheels for the BAGS by Beyer Peacock of Manchester. Finding none at Mar del Plata, we followed a lead that one was working from Maipu but on our arrival there we found only an 11B Class 2-8-0, No.4161, on yard pilot duty, all other engines being either dead or condemned. This included the 12A that stood alongside a 12D Class 4-6-0, one of a class of engine named after Argentinian birds. I had arrived in Argentina with only weeks to spare before the end of steam. I wondered if I would ever find a 12A at work. The whole atmosphere of the BAGS system was so like that of the LNER, not least the red-brick shed buildings, signals and signal boxes.

Somewhat dejectedly we returned to Mar del Plata and took the El Rapido bus to Tandil, the home of the celebrated 11C Class, three-cylinder 4-8-0. However, all we found there was a wheezy 2-6-2T built by Nasmyth Wilson of Patricroft. According to the depot chief at Tandil the only hope of finding an 11C was at Olavarria. The chief also recalled the days when the BAGS engines burnt Welsh coal.

We travelled from Tandil to Olavarria on a wet, stormy Sunday and after checking into our hotel we walked through the streets to the loco shed. There, in the yard, was an 11C, very run down and minus its German-style smoke deflectors. I could have been in Barnsley, the engine was numbered 4222 and was built by Armstrong Whitworth on the Scotswood Road in Newcastle upon Tyne in 1923. She was Argentina's last three-cylinder engine and almost certainly the only three-cylinder 4-8-0 in the world.

On the following day, Monday 18th September 1978, No.4222 worked a cement train on the Loma Negra line. I remember seeing pictures of an 11C taken alongside 'Flying Scotsman' at the Wembley Exhibition in 1924.

Also at Olavaria were several of the wonderful 15B Class 4-8-0s. These Vulcan Foundry giants achieved fame by working the seasonal fruit traffic from the Rio Negro valley to Buenos Aires, a distance of 738 miles. They hauled one thousand-tonne consists on passenger train timings. Over half a million tonnes of fruit were carried in the 1950 season. It will be remembered that it was the British-built railways of Argentina that made her the food basket of the world and also one of the strongest economies in history.

Despite these successes, the lack of a 12A continued to worry me; were there any left? I continued to pursue this with Hector and he agreed to make enquiries across the entire system. Several days later he discovered that one was working in the high-security naval base at Bhia Blanca on the Atlantic coast. The concept of an express passenger engine trundling supplies around a naval base was remarkable but Hector claimed the engine was number 3826, Beyer Peacock 1907, and that was definitely a 12A!

Contact was made with the naval authorities to arrange a visit but the answer was a firm 'No'. Hector mimed that he would be shot if he tried to get us in and he was all set for us to return to Buenos Aires but just before he bought the tickets I had a brainwave. 'Hector, if they won't let us in to see the engine, would they let the engine out?'

By this time nothing surprised him. Mad dogs and Englishmen was a phrase he well understood and I am indebted to him for his persistence because the following day the answer came: 'Yes, for the ridiculous Englishman who has come halfway round the world after a locomotive we will oblige' and arrangements were made for the 12A to be at a local station at 10.00 the following morning.

The engine was astonishingly beautiful with Beyer Peacock, Manchester, England 1907 embossed on a brass plate that curved over the central splasher like a nameplate. Her lineage was pure Great Central and images of industrial Manchester welled up before my eyes despite the bright sunny morning and azure skies of Bhia Blanca. I was really fortunate to be able to capture the essence of that beauty in the half hour we had with the engine before she returned to the naval base and into the history books.

ABOVE The picture made on that unforgettable morning when an Argentinian Railways' 12A Class arrived at Almirante Solier station from the Bahia Blanca naval base. Monday 12th March 1979

RIGHT The last survivor of the Argentinian 11C Class. The first of this class was exhibited at the Wembley Exhibition of 1924, 75 were exported to Argentina

The World's Last 4-4-4Ts, Uruguay

THE MOST HARMONIOUS form of locomotive was the 4-4-4T. The symmetry of this type was matched by the elegance of its Edwardian design. It was a form that flowered briefly. The Wirral Railway had some as did the Metropolitan that worked them as far north as Verney Junction in Northamptonshire on the Oxford to Cambridge line. But these classics of British locomotive design disappeared before the creation of British Railways in 1948 and no examples were preserved.

However, a class of eight beautifully Edwardian-styled 4-4-4Ts continued to work in Uruguay having been built for the Uruguayan Central Railway as their D Class by the Vulcan Foundry at Newton le Willows in Lancashire in 1913.

These engines were one of the highlights of my six-month Latin-American expedition in 1978/9. But the discovery that none was working came as a bitter disappointment and although two were lying in the shed yard at Bella Vista depot in Montevideo, they were in an impossible position for photography purposes. They had a Lancashire & Yorkshire aura fascinatingly combined with a hint of the London Tilbury & Southend 4-4-2Ts. They were derelict and one even had its smokebox completely rusted through. Later it became apparent that they had not worked since the 1950s.

However, all was not lost because there were rumours that others existed as stationary boilers. And so it proved when I found one pumping oil from dockside tanks into wagons for use on the railway system – Uruguay's steam locomotives being oil fired. The engine was locked away inside a small, dark building with the rails truncated past the doorway. Once inside its gloomy interior, I was confronted by a hissing, ghostly apparition in the form of a partly dismembered D Class. The driving wheels were exposed by the removal of the side tanks, the boiler plates were missing and the engine was clad in lagging, the leading wheels had been removed, the front was supported on a wagon bogie and the rear wheels had gone completely. The engine had been converted to wood burning and little wisps of steam appeared at various points although the fire was out. The engine was No.39, built in Lancashire by the Vulcan Foundry as their No.2831 of 1913.

This sadly dismembered hulk was a travesty of the once beautiful D Class and made the ultimate contrast with the 50 or so years these elegant and stylish locomotives had spent working fast suburban trains over the route to Las Piedras and 25 years to de Agosto. The absence of the 4-4-4T in the annals of preservation represents a missing link in the evolution of the British steam locomotive, a doubly regrettable omission when one considers the beauty of this particular form.

On entering the shed's gloomy
interior on Saturday 10th February
1979, I was confronted with the
tantalisingly sad remains of a 4-4-4T,
one of the most elegant forms of
locomotive in railway history

Uruguay

URUGUAY'S RAILWAYS had some of the most delightful British homespun designs ever exported, most of them built by Beyer Peacock in Manchester. It has been suggested that this city's connection with the Fray Bentos meat company was the reason for this. While they were under British ownership, Uruguay's railways were superbly run but after they were handed over to the government in 1960, deterioration set in and by the time of my visit in 1978 the system was in an appallingly rundown condition.

The railway was bankrupt and the state of the permanent way was so bad that speed limits of 12mph were in operation over many stretches. The cancellation of passenger trains was rife and freight traffic was almost non existent, including meat traffic from the huge cattle-rearing plains around Fray Bentos that had once been prolific. A similar situation existed in neighbouring Argentina. I was told on good authority that a fifth column had infiltrated the railway management in Uruguay with the purpose of running down the railway in favour of road development.

Although less than 12 engines were in steam on any one day, a fine variety could be found. Moguls were the mainstay of the fleet such as the N Class from Beyer Peacock that dated back to 1906. But my favourite type was the T Class 2-8-0s. Originally these engines were Moguls supplied by Hawthorn Leslie in 1910 but they were rebuilt into 2-8-0s in 1938 at Uruguay's Penarol Works. They were extremely handsome engines and had a distinct Highland Railway 'Jones' aura about them with their 5ft 2in wheels, long slender boiler, Ramsbottom-type safety valves, rounded cylinders and archaic cab devoid of side windows. The Ts were named after prominent Uruguayan engineers and had their brass nameplates on the side of the firebox – a most unusual practice.

In Florida I found an ancient Beyer Peacock 2-6-0 of 1889 shunting in Piedra Alta wagon works. A wheezy veteran in the truest sense, she had slide valves and was coupled to an outside-frame tender of the same year that looked as if it had been taken off a Midland Railway Kirtley 0-6-0.

Walking around the shed at Paysandu on a wet and windy summer evening in 1978, I found the entire allocation that included seven different classes, had come from Beyer Peacock. One of these was the last surviving Z Class 2-8-0. This veteran had a typical L&NW front, reminiscent of Whale's 2-8-0s of World War One and contrasted superbly with the ever-present N Class Moguls with their basic Edwardian appearance and hint of Scottish ancestry.

On Sunday afternoons at Paysandu shed the silence was broken only by the clatter of pigeons in the rafters and the dripping of water from the dead engines. I remember the sun streaming through the broken slats of the old depot roof covering the two T Class 2-8-0s in mottles as the engines stood side by side exuding a rich aroma of cold soot. It might have been a Scottish depot in the highlands in the 1920s.

However, it wasn't just the locomotives. The atmosphere at Montevideo's Central Articas station evoked powerful feelings of the past. It was almost impossible not to think one was in St Pancras, so similar was the architecture. The entrance to Central Articas station included statues of James Watt and George Stephenson. The awe-inspiring architecture of this station evoked a tranquil atmosphere of timelessness. When bustling activity can be combined with an overriding tranquillity civilisation reigns supreme.

Tragically this magnificent railway was on the very brink of destruction.

LEFT The T Class 2-8-0s were my favourite Uruguayan class and here No.139 'Ing Pedro Magnou' is seen leaving Paysandu with a mixed freight

BOTTOM A night session at Paysandu on Saturday 17th February 1979 produced this picture of the last surviving Uruguayan Railway's Z Class 2-6-0 No.225, built by Beyer Peacock of Manchester in 1929. I particularly liked the 'North-Western'-style front of these engines, seen here with some characteristic 'North-Western' animation to match

The moment of triumph at Taltal
when the world's last Kitson Meyer
returned to life

The Dodo of the Atacama Desert, Chile

ON REACHING SANTIAGO I sought information about the last articulated Kitson Meyer that operated from the Pacific port of Taltal in the Atacama desert hundreds of miles to the north. The Chilean Ministry of Chemicals and Minerals said the railway had closed and was being dismantled. This was a bitter blow but I was determined to go and to record whatever was left.

When I arrived in Taltal in February 1979 it was like a Nevada ghost town with partly dismantled buildings, abandoned jetties, derelict store sheds and rusted sidings. This was all that was left of the many British-owned gold and nitrate railways that led from the waterless interior of the desert to various ports along Chile's Pacific coast. The rough terrain demanded articulated locomotives and Kitson of Leeds supplied their 0-6-6-0 Kitson Meyers, an articulated predecessor of the Garratt type.

But everything I saw in Taltal told me that it was too late. The Victorian house of the former general manager still stood as proud as ever overlooking the works but most of the track had been lifted. The large engine shed, that had had a capacity for 30 locomotives had been pulled down.

All around were pieces of cut-up Kitson Meyers. Time clocks still adorned the office walls and in a heap of dust and old papers lay a 'Girls Annual' of 1912 – what an incomparable industrial past Britain has.

After supper at the residencia, the landlady came in and asked me to follow a small boy to a nearby house from where the sounds of a Chopin piano sonata floated from the open windows. It was the home of Eric Ridpeth, 'you are just in time for the BBC World Service' he announced. Eric was 80 having been born in Tottenham in 1899. He came to Chile in 1921 to work with Anglo Chilean Nitrates and had lived in Taltal ever since.

'There's no railway here,' was Eric's retort to my question about the Kitson Meyers, 'only a wreck. I spent my life with that railway, it was one of the finest in the world.' But miraculously Eric did confirm that one Kitson Meyer was left, standing down by the beach. 'Senor Acosta, the last manager, used it on demolition work but

it's as rotten as a pear and will never work again.' I couldn't sleep for excitement and first thing the following morning I was banging on Acosta's door and soon I was taken to see the engine. It was No.59 and she stood dumped on a line next to the beach.

The engine was one of the most exciting discoveries I had ever made, the last survivor of a link in an evolutionary chain of articulated locomotives. My heart pounded as I imagined the engine coming to life and with a slightly trembling voice I asked Acosta, 'Can it be steamed?' I was told it could if some repairs were made. There was abundant technical labour available in Taltal and if I paid the expenses they would steam the engine. I went back to Eric's house to tell him joyfully what had been arranged but he would have nothing to do with it. 'Leave it alone' he said. 'I told you the boiler is as rotten as a pear. It will blow up on Acosta, you will see!'

An 11.30 next morning Acosta announced that they were ready to light the fire. My journey halfway round the world had borne fruit. Swirls of dark oil smoke gushed from the engine's front chimney while shrouds of pure white steam issued from the rear. Then, without warning, a geyser of scalding water escaped from the leading chimney and the engine disappeared in a huge ball of steam and water.

At the heart of the affray I noticed a tall elderly figure silently watching through a distant gate. But Acosta was unrepentant; 'it will take another day,' he said, 'we must let her cool down first'.

The following afternoon the engine was in steam again but after only a few minutes a strange, throaty, bubbling sound intensified into a roar and once again the engine disappeared in a ball of steam. Acosta's eyes were full of defiance. 'We will repair it tomorrow,' he said calmly.

Sure enough 48 hours later, the Meyer had steam yet again. The veteran picked up some wagons and headed away through the derelict works towards Breas. It was as if the whole of Taltal had come to life once again, No.59's lovely chime whistle blew plaintively around the hills, a sound guaranteed to strike a chord in the heart of every resident. Young and old alike flocked to the old works area to see the engine resurrected. It was a triumph of determination to reach that wild place, a triumph of a railway manager determined to respond to a challenge and the triumph of the steam locomotive to turn a wheel no matter how great the odds. Now the final triumph was to be mine, as I put this unique locomotive onto film.

The syncopated exhaust beat of the Kitson Meyer echoed around Taltal's lonely hills as the engine, later to be known by the 'Sunday Times' as 'The Dodo of the Atacama' breathed its final gasps.

ABOVE The Dodo of Chile's Atacama Desert. This solitary engine outlived all of its sisters and survived in this desert sanctuary until 1978, having spent 70 years hauling nitrate and gold from the interior of the desert to the port of Taltal

LEFT Classic British lineage in the form of Taltal's Kitson Meyer

Ludlow Jute Mill, Calcutta

DURING A MEETING WITH Mike Satow at the time he was setting up India's National Railway Museum, he asked me if I knew about the fireless engines at Ludlow Jute Mills in Calcutta. I didn't know about them but took careful notes ready for my next visit to India.

I arrived at Ludlow in December 1979 having been working with the blue XC at Burdwan. Ludlow was located on the South Eastern Railways' Kharagpur line close to Chengail station and only a few miles past Santraganchi shed. The Ludlow Jute Mills were located in an idyllic setting on the west bank of the Hooghly river south of Calcutta. It reminded me of Cadbury's factory in a garden at Bournville that I had visited as a child, except that Ludlow was even more beautiful. I was given excellent accommodation at the factory guest house during my four-day stay. Crows and egrets roosted in the surrounding trees, kingfishers inhabited the factory pond and Woodpeckers were in evidence along with many species of butterfly.

The mill was a sanctuary in teeming Calcutta with its clean air and beautiful wooded views of the mighty Hooghly. It was a healthy place and there seemed a high level of contentment. A few people working hard in a beautiful environment was perhaps the perfect recipe for contentment. Ships from all parts of the world sailed past going to and from Calcutta docks. Sunrise on the river was an event to be savoured as the golden morning mist slowly dispersed to reveal the smoking brickwork chimneys over on the east bank.

Ever since 1923 fireless engines have flitted around the factory bringing raw materials from the jetty on the river. The two engines working there were both 0-4-0s from Orenstein and Koppel but of fascinatingly different design. Ludlow No.1 had its chimney and cylinders to the rear and the regulator valve combined with the handle in the cab. The engine was Orenstein and Koppel No.10478, Berlin Drewitz-built in 1923 and presumably received new by the mill. Ludlow No.3 had her cylinders placed to the front and had a conventional chimney. This engine's plate bore the inscription 'Parrys Engineers as sole agent for Orenstein and Koppel in India'. No works number was given.

These engines were a judicious choice for industries such as jute where sparks from a conventional locomotive could easily have caused fires.

Sunset over the Hooghly as a
Fireless engine draws a rake of
raw jute for processing at the mill

LEFT Double-headed Fireless as Ludlow Jute Mill's two Orenstein and Koppel 0-4-0Fs ease a rake of raw material over the jetty and into the factory

BELOW Fireless locomotives are ideal in works or factories that have a ready supply of steam. This is injected at high pressure into the storage vessel on the engine and fed to the cylinders via a reducing valve to achieve a constant power output. Often likened to a Thermos flask on wheels, a Fireless engine is a prudent choice for industries such as jute, where sparks from a conventional engine could cause fires

The dung girls of Khatauli set out
pats of bullock dung to dry as
'Cheetal' trundles past with a rake
of freshly cut sugar cane

Indian Sugar Fields

A FINE VARIETY OF MOTIVE POWER operated on the sugar plantations of northern India. Many of the mills operated 2ft gauge for bringing in the cane and one meter for connecting with Indian Railways' main lines. The lines around the factories usually were of mixed gauge. It was hoped that the sugar railways would continue in operation after steam ended on Indian Railways as had happened in many other countries but this was not to be. In fact rather the opposite occurred and the sugar lines had all but finished by the end of the 20th century.

In 1979 two Indian sugar mills had the oldest working steam locomotives in the world in the form of 'Tweed' and 'Mersey'. These were meter-gauge D Class 0-4-0s built at Sharp Stewart's Great Bridgewater Street works, Manchester in 1873. 'Tweed' worked at Suraya Mill near Gorakhpur and was supported by a roster of 2ft 6in-gauge veterans including a 4-4-0 from Vulcan Foundry, 1884, and a delightful Kitson 0-6-2 of 1900. 'Mersey' worked at SKG Mills, Hathua, in association with Baldwin 2ft-gauge 4-6-0Ts that were former military engines of World War One. Motipur sugar factory had a meter-gauge mixed-traffic Class E 0-4-2 that was ex-Bombay Baroda and Central India Railway. This veteran bore a Vulcan Foundry plate dated 1877.

I covered all these mills in December 1979 but never got to Lohat where the last of the legendary F Class 0-6-0s could be found. This standard meter-gauge type totalled 870 locomotives built between 1884 and 1922 by 12 different builders including Ajmer Works in India.

Diminutive by most standards, the F Class weighed between 20 and 24 tonnes in full working order. The type is famous in world locomotive history and the failure to record this last survivor had become a source of great disappointment to me.

Two years after my adventures with 'Tweed' and 'Mersey' I visited the Upper India Sugar Mill at Khatauli in The United Provinces where a delightful 2ft-gauge 0-4-0WT, built by John Fowler's works in Leeds in 1923 and named 'Cheetal', worked turn about with two Baldwin War Department 4-6-0s of World War One. The system based at Khatauli included a lengthy run of about 12 miles out into the fields, a journey that revealed a great diversity of Indian village life.

One of the best pictures from my week-long visit in February 1981 was 'Dung Girl' that shows girls as young as 12 collecting bullock dung from the highways, mixing it into cakes and piling it into turrets to dry for use as domestic heating and domestic cooking fuel. As the girls pile up the dung from ladders leaning against the stack 'Cheetal' smokily hurries past with a long rake of freshly cut cane. As recently as the 1970s, the bullock was the largest mover of tonnage on the Indian sub-continent – second only to Indian Railways. The dung girls made a fine contrast to 'Cheetal' crossing a small river viaduct as the local pig farmer waters his herd in the river below. This picture was laced with the golden sunlight of an Indian winter afternoon and while I was waiting for 'Cheetal' to appear the calls of wild peacocks could be heard in the adjacent thickets.

A couple of thousand vultures were said to live in the immediate vicinity of Khatauli and could be seen daily on the ground, in trees and on buildings. They constituted one of the world's great ornithological sights. There was a bone-processing factory manufacturing fertiliser at Khatauli and a group of low-caste Hindus brought in dead animals from miles around. Vultures would strip the skeletons by tearing at the rotting flesh in an eerie and chilling way. The subsequent rattle of bones as they squabbled about the pecking order was characterised by their hideous cackle. To see hundreds of these birds gliding on their wide swooping wings was an amazing spectacle. As 'Cheetal' left the engine sheds each morning it passed a gnarled lineside tree that invariably played host to a large flock of vultures. It took me several mornings to achieve the necessary dexterity to obtain a picture of 'Cheetal' and the vultures without the birds flying away.

ABOVE Suraya Sugar Mill's splendid chocolate liveried 2ft 6in-gauge 0-6-2T, No.54, built by Kitson of Leeds in 1900, at a cane loading siding on Sunday 9th January 1977

LEFT Worksplate of the Kitson 0-6-2 at Suraya

TOP LEFT 'Cheetal' and the pig farmer

BOTTOM LEFT Dated Sunday 8th February 1981, this picture shows ex-World War One Baldwin 4-6-0 No.1 of 1917 at the head of a loaded sugar cane train on the Upper India Mills system at Khatauli. It also features a village elder, pats of bullock dung drying in the sun, a sleeping dog and a brass bucket.

The Greek Graveyards

FOR ME LOCOMOTIVE GRAVEYARDS have always been an important aspect of documenting 'The Last Steam Locomotives of the World'. Graveyards often include long-obsolete types that otherwise would never have been covered. The sites also can be very photogenic and full of atmosphere.

Graveyards can be either mature or recent. The really mature ones invariably offer the best potential and the site where three Forneys lie in the mouth of the Solomon river in Alaska, represents the epitome of a mature site, having been there for upwards of a hundred years. This site also has a special historical interest because it contains the last steam locomotives of North America.

In contrast, the dump at Barry Island that contained the last steam locomotives of Great Britain, was not a mature site, either in terms of vegetation or of large amounts of rust, and the engines were pushed tightly together. Despite its relevance historically, it was not photogenic and very few really good pictures ever came from there.

The standard-gauge graveyards on the Greek mainland were perhaps the closest to perfection one could get. They met every possible criteria, they contained historic locomotives including British and American classics from World War Two, along with designs that were derived from Karl Golsdorf's creations for the Austro-Hungarian Empire. The engines were spread over a wide area, often with trees and bushes growing between them and for many months of the year the sites were covered with wild flowers. Two principal locations existed, most importantly the old station dump at Thessaloniki and secondly the one at the former locomotive depot at Tithorea.

But this was not all, for by the late 1970s, the extensive meter-gauge network on the Peloponnese peninsular held a number of mature graveyards, one with an outstanding location. It was situated at Acladokampos on a section of the meter-gauge line to Kalamata.

The line originally made a long horseshoe curve around a valley but this section became disused when a viaduct was built to avoid the horseshoe.

The disused section of main line then became an ideal place to dump abandoned locomotives that had been gathered from all over the network. To see a long line of rusty engines in magnificent isolation high up on a mountainside was unforgettable.

The dump contained many of the archaic-looking Z Class 2-6-0s introduced by Societe Alsacienne Graffenstaden of France in 1890. It also held some of the famous MacArthur 2-8-2s of World War Two, a type that has seen widespread service in many countries. One of the rusted MacArthurs had two derelict wagons behind it and at twilight the combination looked like a ghost train when seen against the surrounding amphitheatre of hills and spiky vegetation.

I spent six days at Acladokampos in August 1982, having found frugal accommodation in a village several miles away. The weather was very hot and most nights I preferred to sleep outside under the stars. I would rise at dawn because getting to the dump involved a long walk through olive groves and I always wanted to be at my chosen location ready for the early morning light. By 0900 the sun had become too strident for much creative work.

Some very satisfying photography was done during that spell. It included looking down from a rocky overhang on two Zs bathed in early rippling light. Another view was from the valley floor showing dumped engines up on the mountainside. But the rarest theme was of a rusty MacArthur with thistles in the foreground, a railcar crossing the viaduct in the background and Acladokampos village visible in the blue haze of the far distance.

It was a study that captured the atmosphere of the place to perfection.

TOP LEFT The old station dump at Thessaloniki

ABOVE A late-afternoon study at Acladokampos Mountain dump with Breda 2-8-2 No.7112 and Linke Hoffman 2-8-0 No.7725

ABOVE An abandoned meter-gauge Z Class on the Peloponnese peninsula

TOP Two Greek meter-gauge Z Class 2-6-0s lie abandoned on the Peloponnese peninsular on Sunday 15th August 1982

ABOVE Kalamata: Greek Railways' Z Class 2-6-0 No.7544 lies abandoned. Monday 9th April 1973

FAR LEFT A Golsdorf-inspired 0-10-0 on the dump at Thessaloniki

LEFT A similarly inspired 2-10-0 on the dump at Thessaloniki in October 1979

CENTRE A spider in its lair

LEFT The old station dump at Thessaloniki on Monday 30th August 1982

LEFT Greek Railways' meter-gauge Z Class 2-6-0 No.7509 abandoned at Pirgos on Sunday 8th April 1973

China, Mainline Operation

BEFORE CHINA OPENED its borders to visitors it was popularly believed that many rare types of locomotive existed there. Were any of the beautiful Kerr Stuart Singles, exported in 1910 and bedecked in Imperial yellow livery as mail engines, still on the Shanghai to Nanking route? Or were there any Dean Goods, known to have been sent there as part of wartime operations? The reality was very different and when the Bamboo Curtain was finally lifted a high level of standardisation, second only to that of Russian Railways, was found. These two communist nations with their strict central-government policies, devoid of the free-enterprise capitalist system, found it logical to standardise on a massive scale.

As recently as the 1980s it was estimated that China had about 11,000 steam locomotives in active service. Five main line types were in operation: QJ, 2-10-2s; JS and JF Mikados; RM and SL6 Pacifics. By far the most numerous were the QJs, of which more than 5,000 were built. However, what was lost by the paucity of different designs was partially made up for by the density of traffic on the main lines, along with the embellishments applied to many of the locomotives. China's most beautifully decked examples rivalled the most flamboyant designs from the golden age of steam.

China's steam-worked main lines became well known during the 1980s and early 1990s. One of the principal routes for steam was from Harbin, the capital of Heilongjing Province, south westwards through Manchuria to Beijing, via the industrialised cities of Changchun and Shenyang. This route was one of the busiest steam-worked lines in railway history, the endless succession of freights, with trains passing every 15 minutes truly brought the steam age back to life. Some routes could be even busier and I recall one stint on the lineside between Shenyang and Dalian when, for several continuous hours, there were QJs hauling 2,000-tonne freight trains heading southwards on average every nine minutes. The thrusting growth of China in all its vastness, with one quarter of the human race within its borders, makes for massive transport logistics and this situation was paralleled by the extensive building of railways in China in contrast to all other parts of the world.

Steam seemed destined to have a long-term future in China. A political target of achieving a thermal efficiency of 15 per cent had been set by the government and many experiments were made to improve efficiency, particularly with the QJs.

China had abundant quantities of iron, coal, water and labour and the trusty steam locomotive, with all its in-built simplicity and longevity, seemed destined to last well into the 21st century. However, a radical change in policy came about when some autonomy was given to the various railway bureaux who decided to move away from central-government policy and look towards more modern forms of motive power. By the 1990s China had reversed its policy, having come to regard the steam locomotive increasingly as an outmoded aspect of the smoke-stack age from which the country wished to distance itself.

Steam production at Datong was halted in favour of building diesels and a rapid run down of steam occurred during the 1990s in a way similar to how the same thing happened in Britain during the 1960s.

Some of my finest memories of main-line action in China were during my late summer sessions at the summit of Wangang Bank south of Harbin on the Manchurian main line. These took place over several years during the group tours I did for Occidor in the 1980s and early 1990s. We would spend the whole day there. A mini-bus would leave the hotel in Harbin at 07.30 with photographic equipment, lunch boxes and flasks of boiling water piled on board. To reach the summit from the road we passed over several crop fields full of aubergines, peppers,

A China Railways' JS Class 2-8-2 climbs Nancha Bank, one of the great attractions of Chinese main-line steam in its final years, with a passenger train for Yichun. It is being banked up the incline by a tender-first QJ 2-10-2. Diesels finally took over in the mid-1990s

tomatoes and cucumbers, all at their peak of ripeness. By 08.30 we would be on location. The mini-bus would return at 17.00, giving us eight hours on the busiest steam-worked line in the world.

The line's direction was roughly from north to south, making the east bank good for morning work and after a midday break when the sun was high, the west bank was good until the shadows lapped onto the rails at 16.30 in the afternoon. A constant succession of trains smokily laboured their way up the bank. The engine crews were amazed to see so many foreigners wielding cameras and tripods. Some girls had set up a coffee cum picnic area beneath adjacent trees. Everyone was hoping for a masterpiece but there were so many variables for any given train: the condition of the engine, the amount of smoke and steam or a fortuitous twist of exhaust, the angle of light and, of course, the type of consist the

engine had, some rakes being much more photogenic than others. Added to this were the focal length of the lens and the position of the camera and the ability to get the train in exactly the right position. All these factors combined to make a heady mix. The star engine was QJ Class No.2470 named 'Zhou De'; the pride of Harbin. This engine was kept in immaculate trim. It carried a huge brass plate on its smoke box door depicting General Zhou De and was one of China's few named locomotives. A Harbin engine for many years, we usually saw 'Zhou De' at least once on each lineside day.

It was a privileged situation, we could afford to let a train pass if the engine were too dirty or not showing sufficient exhaust. We had the same advantages lineside photographers had had during the golden years of steam who were able to sit at the trackside in contemplative leisure and take only the scenes that inspired them most.

ABOVE A China Railways SL6 Class Pacific heads southwards from Anshan with a stopping train from Shenyang to Dalian. Specially planted lineside blooms are a delightful aspect of China Railways. They extend for hundreds of miles

ABOVE A China Railway's SL6 Class Pacific passes Saddle Mountain south of Anshan with a stopping train from Dalian to Shenyan

RIGHT In temperatures of -20C a China Railways QJ Class 2-10-2 battles its way up Nancha Bank with a southbound passenger train from Yichun

The Magnificent Pt47s, Poland

A REMARKABLE THREE-WEEK SOJOURN, living in a motor caravan on a bridge on a farm in Poland formed the operational base for recording Poland's Pt47 Class Mikados. The bridge was located on the Kamieniec to Klodsko section of the international main line from Wrocslaw to Prague. It was June/July 1983 and the line carried 16 steam passenger trains a day, all hauled by Pt47s.

The bridge was at Byczen, just south of Kamieniec. To the north was a superb cutting, partly wooded and about a mile long. The line's direction was north to south, providing both morning and afternoon locations. I got to know the cutting intimately, every tree and every shadow. Favourite picture locations emerged and were given names like 'New Willow', 'Daisy Bank', 'Bunting Branch', 'Smoky Bridge' etc.

A friendship was established with the local farmer who brought his cows up daily for grazing and I was kept well supplied with milk, eggs and fruit, including the largest red cherries imaginable. Turtle Doves purred in the lazy heat and the scratchy song of the Whitethroat could always be heard. Quail called from the fields. Green Woodpeckers shrieked their strident yaffle from a lineside coppice while deer fed from a crop of young peas next to the bridge.

It was a rural paradise; fields of haystacks, huge cart horses and colourful field workers – old women bent double and farm labourers like the rustic figures in Cezanne's 'Card players'. There were glimpses of Corot in the meandering brooks and willow trees, backed by the orange-roofed houses of Byczen. Here was rural Poland, safe, peaceful and totally unspoiled. In the evenings I would sit in the advancing twilight listening to the Owls and after dark a Nightingale would sing and I was lulled to sleep on many nights by his soft melodies.

Aesthetically, the Pt47s were true period pieces despite being relatively new engines – all of them were built between the late 1940s and early 1950s. They were almost identical to the larger Pu29 of the late 1920s. Cegielski of Poznan built 60 Pt47s and Chrzanow built 120.

Pt47s are important historically because they are the finest surviving examples of the Polish school of locomotive design that flowered after the First World War when Poland emerged as a united and self-governing country. Before this Poland was annexed between Germany, Austria and Russia.

The following extract is taken from my diary dated Sunday 19th June 1983. 'The Klodsko to Katowice express passed this evening in epic style; Pt47 No.113, with lamps blazing and a massive roar of exhaust issuing a

mighty cloud of grey smoke into the atmosphere. With steam spouting noisily from her cylinder cocks, she burst under the bridge, totally enveloping us in smoke as the 12-coach train thundered beneath.

'The cutting was filled with sulphurous emanations that hung in the air for several minutes afterwards, sweet smelling and evocative in the pure evening air.

'Recent rain had made the atmosphere clear, amplifying the throbbing rhythms as the train receded through the wet countryside. Minutes later a Ty2 – a German war engine – came the other way and no sooner had it passed than a Bunting began to sing a plaintive little song from the bushes by the path'.

Just south of the bridge was a section of railway I called 'little shap' on account of it being almost a miniature version of Britain's legendary Shap Bank.

LEFT A Polish Railways' Class Pt47, 2-8-2 near 'Smoky Bridge' during my sojourn at Byczen in July 1983

ABOVE Another Class Pt47, 2-8-2 passes 'New Willow' location with a northbound express in July 1983

The Last Feldbahn

MY EXPEDITION to the primeval woodlands of Baliostok in north-eastern Poland close to the Russian border, was to locate the last working Feldbahn, the German military engine of World War One. These historic 600mm-gauge locomotives were built in huge numbers as part of Germany's war effort and were extensively used in war theatres, including bringing supplies up to the front line. At the end of the conflict they were surplus to military requirements and many were pensioned off into industrial service.

On reaching Baliostok, I was told that Feldbahns operated at nearby Czarna but when I arrived there I was confronted with the Feldbahn graveyard, ten of them were lying in an overgrown dump. However, my guide disappeared into the site offices and returned smiling and gesticulating: 'One of them is still working, it's coming in with a long train'.

Sure enough, within an hour clouds of steam announced the arrival of Feldbahn TX, No.1117, built by Henschel of Cassel in 1918. Feldbahns were built by at least 11 different makers and the class totalled about 2,500 locomotives in total. Their long wheelbase, necessitated by eight coupled wheels, was made flexible by Klien-Linder axles at front and rear. Their weight in working order was only 12½ tonnes. The engine I had located at Czarna was almost certainly the last working survivor.

Of all the locomotive designs in history, war engines came closest to becoming international in their distribution because invariably they were built in large numbers and were surplus to requirements once the conflict ended.

The Allied forces' equivalent to the Feldbahn during World War One were built in America because British foundries were under great pressure producing munitions. Two designs were prepared, first was a 4-6-0T and later a 2-6-2T. Both types were built in large numbers and were also widely distributed after the conflict, some being sent to the sugar plantations of India.

ABOVE A Feldbahn on the dump at Czarna Bialostocka seen through the smashed spectacle glasses of a sister engine. May 1983

RIGHT The last working Feldbahn emerges from the woods at Czarna Bialostocka at the head of a loaded log train. May 1983

China, Iron and Steel

MANY OF CHINA'S surviving steam locomotives are in iron and steel works and appropriately so, as it is now two centuries since the world's first steam locomotive was born in a Welsh ironworks. Perhaps the most dramatic location today is Baotou in Inner Mongolia that has an allocation of 24 SYs, although at the time of my visit in March 2005 dieselisation was progressing. The works are one of China's largest and form the principal industry of this vast city that lies on the edge of the mountainous Aubuqi Desert about 30 miles to the southwest. The raw ironstone for the complex is taken from the mountain range to the north. A vast network of lines exist in and around the works and the clamour cannot be easily endured for long – heat, dust and noise being all-pervading.

However, the most dramatic combination of steam and steel in China occurred at Anshan, China's steel capital, some 45 miles from Shenyang on the main line to Dalian. Sadly, Anshan has dieselised over recent years but when I first went there in January 1984 it had a roster of about 40 steam locomotives embracing six different classes, three Mikado, two Prairie and some ex-United States Army 0-6-0Ts from World War Two. This roster reflected the kind of motive power one might have found in a similar complex in America three quarters of a century ago.

On my arrival in Anshan I was met by Zhou Yongli who announced that I was the second English visitor to arrive within a few days, my visit following that of David Blunkett and his Sheffield City Councillors who had visited Anshan to twin the two cities. Zhou had guided the party and spoke well of Sheffield's blind leader, his good humour and intellect and of the economic and cultural links they intended to forge. Nowhere on Earth could be more appropriate for Anshan to be associated with and I thought of the days when Sheffield was at its industrial height and known as 'hell with the lid off'.

Production on the Anshan complex was an unbelievable 13.85 million tonnes of iron and steel a year and the activities necessary to produce this total had to be seen to be believed. Six different factories make up the site including ten blast furnaces, three steel mills, a sinter plant, a huge coking plant, 20 rolling mills, two power stations, a refractory and a machine repair shop.

The area is surrounded by rich deposits of iron ore that is brought into the works by a circular electric railway. China Railways also bring in phenomenal tonnages of other commodities including coal mainly from Fushun, scrap metal, limestone, magnesium and all the materials necessary to keep the complex in good repair and in a constant state of development, 17.5 million tonnes of iron and steel was the targeted production for 1990.

Anshan's output includes cast iron, steel billets, shaped steel, steel sheets, strips, girders, rails, tubes and wires. Some items go direct to Dalian for export but most were for domestic use, including pig iron and steel for the steam-locomotive works in Datong in Inner Mongolia.

I was particularly fascinated by Steel Mill No.1 where a bank of flaming, open-hearth furnaces reminded me of the words written by James Nasmyth, inventor of the steam hammer, following a visit he made to the Black Country in the 1830s. Nasmyth described 'smut-covered, white-eyed men who dashed between the flames against a roaring cacophony of furnaces and clanging mills'.

There, directly in front of my camera, seemed the epitome of Nasmyth's words and the essence of the industrial revolution.

A moment of sheer delight at Baotou Iron and Steel Works as three SY Class Mikados assemble in the depot yard between turns of duty. Monday 7th March 2005

ABOVE A Chinese industrial SY
Class Mikado is coaled by a
mobile conveyer at Baotou Iron
and Steel Works in March 2005

RIGHT The scrap line at the Baotou
works contained several Polish
ET7 Class 0-8-0Ts. These worked
at Baotou before being replaced
by SYs. Tuesday 8th March 2005

FAR RIGHT On the same bitterly
cold day at the Baotou works, the
low-angle winter sunlight
produced this reflective study of
the driving wheels of SY Class
2-8-2 No.3012 as she left the
works after mechanical attention

My notes from Baotou Iron and Steel Works relating to this picture read as follows: 'Loco works 'overhaul' SY Class No.1431 under repair with afternoon sunlight at 16.30 filtering through the windows and illuminating the wheels and the boiler'

TOP LEFT AND RIGHT The main slag bank at Anshan Iron and Steel Works was a source of great pictorial drama as the SYs brought the cauldrons of waste for tipping, often the waste was fully molten and the searing heat could be felt from over a hundred yards away

BOTTOM LEFT Industrial "shepherd" at Anshan governing the flow of molten waste from the blast furnaces

BOTTOM RIGHT Steel Mill No.1 at Anshan consisted of a bank of flaming, open hearth furnaces which dated back to Japanese times. They were fabulous to watch in operation and equally absorbing to photograph

ABOVE An SY Class industrial 2-8-2 in golden afternoon sunlight against the blast furnaces at Anshan

RIGHT Anshan was exceptional in having several of these rare industrial Prairie 2-8-2s. Here, No.290, classified YJ, is seen alongside blast furnace No.2

Building the World's Last Steam Locomotives, Datong Works

NEVER WILL I FORGET the emotions I experienced on entering Datong Works on the edge of Inner Mongolia in January 1984. The sight that confronted me evoked a trance-like situation, the vast shop contained 20 or more boilers in various stages of construction. Inner and outer fireboxes contrasted with boiler shells, all illuminated and silhouetted in ghostly patterns by the welders' blinding flashes and set to a deafening cacophony of heavy drilling. Two classes were being built: the JS general purpose 2-8-2 and the QJ heavy freight 2-10-2. At that particular time the emphasis was on JS production and two locomotives a day were being assembled.

I had never seen labour so brilliantly organised or working so feverishly. Engines were manifested from nothing within a matter of a few hours. What would be a naked frame at lunchtime would be transformed before one's eyes into a fully fledged locomotive during the course of the afternoon so that by 18.00 the complete engine, painted in orange undercoat, would be wheeled out to the steam-testing sheds. Absolutely unbelievable!

The Chinese were justifiably proud of their enterprise and the frenzied activities at Datong were expressed succinctly by my guide when he turned to me and confided: 'Our workers move like Charlie Chaplin did in your old films'.

My excitement was intensified by the knowledge that many of Datong's locomotives were being sent to new lines as railway construction continued apace in China. It was true to say that China was building steam railways not just locomotives. I remember thinking what an invigorating situation this was because at that time railways were quite widely discredited. But the Chinese had the good sense to say 'we have no motorways but we have the iron, coal, water and labour so we can build one modern steam locomotive for approximately one seventh of the cost of an equivalent diesel'.

Datong Works covered an area of 2.32 million square meters and in addition to the manufacturing processes were the domestic, living and social facilities for the 95 per cent of the 8,600 strong workforce who lived within the complex.

In addition to the 23 manufacturing workshops there were five schools, a hospital, a 2,200 seat auditorium, a library, sports grounds, recreation rooms and a kindergarten.

Datong has a mixed workforce on almost all duties and it was amazing to see a huge JS being moved onto its wheels in the erecting shop by cranes driven by teenage girls. In the casting shop we spoke to one of Datong's young female workers. Her name was Duan Aiping, she was 24 and employed making up the sand moulds for the leading wheels of the JS Class. She loved the work and didn't recognise any monotony in her task. 'Each small part is integral to the whole,' she told me. 'And I feel proud when I see the locomotives running on the line because they are working for the advancement of our country'. I couldn't help but contrast Aiping's sentiments with those one might hear from her counterparts in the west whose work priorities might well revolve around wages, convenient hours and closeness to home etc.

One of the most remarkable parts of Datong Works was the cavernous steam-testing shed in which about six engines, still in workshop orange, stood under varying pressures of steam. The atmosphere created by the orange giants sitting in the gloom was positively eerie and so intense was their presence that I felt as if I had entered a cave full of living dinosaurs.

In 1969 I had begun a race against time to document the 'Last Steam Locomotives of the World' and here, 15 years later, I found myself in a vast works that was producing 280 steam locomotives a year – some that might well outlive me.

RIGHT A newly constructed JS Class Mikado stands in the gloom of the steam-testing shed at Datong

RIGHT A hoarding extols the workers to 'Follow the Safety Rules'

FAR RIGHT Firebox welding

TOP Sand moulds for wheels in the casting shop

ABOVE Precision measurements being taken on the driving axle of a QJ

TOP Preparing rough cylinder castings

ABOVE A coal-gas bleeder pipe directed into a holed drum

RIGHT A smoky corner of the works

TOP The late afternoon sunlight filters through the windows of the erecting shop to illuminate a QJ under construction

ABOVE QJ Class driving wheels prior to being rolled beneath a locomotive

185

China – on shed

BIG STEAM DEPOTS with allocations of a hundred locomotives have disappeared and their like will never be seen again. The sheer, awesome presence of dozens of locomotives in such close proximity was one of the most exciting aspects of the steam age. Large steam depots survived in China until the late 1980s at Su ja Tun in Shenyang, along with the depots at Changchun and Harbin. These three running sheds provided motive power for the intensely busy main line through Manchuria from Harbin in the northeast either to the Yellow Sea port of Dalian or to Beijing. The Manchurian main line passed through China's most industrialised regions.

In the mid-1980s Su ja Tun's allocation reflected China's rigid standardisation policy by having only five types allocated: JF and JS Mikados; QJ, 2-10-2s and two Pacifics, RMs and SL6. During those final years of main-line steam when the engines were heavily utilised, they would come on shed to have their fires tended, be coaled and watered, have their sandboxes topped up and oiling done and several hours later be back on the main line with another train.

Changchun had an allocation of 78 engines, 50 were QJs. The running shed was complimented by a huge locomotive works and a vast rolling-stock plant. Close to 150 miles north of Changchun lies Harbin, gem of the northeast and capital of Heilongjiang Province. Harbin's huge marshalling yards formed a clearing house for traffic to and from the far northeast. Harbin also provided the motive power, the constant stream of locomotives arriving and leaving the shed was a revelation as was the intensity of the servicing operation on the ash-pit roads. On the Manchurian main line, Harbin engines worked as far as Wujiatze, where Changchun engines took over.

Some of China's smaller locomotive sheds were also very exciting particularly those whose interiors were an exotic mixture of sunlight smoke and shadow. By far the most dramatic of these was the old steam depot at Anshan Iron and Steel Works where vibrant bands of sunlight filtered into the depot and reacted with the smoke and steam coming from the engines inside. The ever-changing patterns of the locomotives, moving around in semi darkness and gangs of men in silhouette, provided a tapestry of constant change and fascination. I spent two days in that enchanted place with seldom a dull moment.

A similar but rather more subtle variation happened at Nampiao in March 2005. An SY had come on shed for attention to its valve gear. A few pale rays seeped into the depot and there was a pool of light on the floor in the middle distance but nothing of sufficient contrast or atmospheric enough to create a picture.

That was until the engine received a much-needed round of coal. The smoke oozed silently from the crippled locomotive and on reaching the roof spread out to fill the whole roof area and eventually the entire depot. As the sunlight caught the smoke it transformed it into rich potions of malleable tone and colour. Two passing workmen stopped to chat in the sun spot and a third man joined them moments later.

In an instant the entire scene came to life: atmosphere, colour, contrast, the interaction of men and machines and the picture was completed by looking along the side of the engine and into the shed to where the three men stood.

LEFT Whilst setting up the camera for this picture of an SY Class Mikado on the Nampiao coal system three workmen suddenly appeared and stood talking for a few seconds - just long enough to make this interesting correlation between man and machine.

BELOW On shed. One of Baotou Iron and Steel Works' 24 SY Class industrial Mikados

LEFT Sunlight, smoke and shadow at the running shed at Anshan Iron and Steel Works. This busy depot once had about 50 steam locomotives allocated to it, although many were sub-shedded out to servicing points around the complex. Engines were coming and going around the clock whenever detailed repairs had to be made that could not be carried out at the sub depots. Here, SYs and a solitary Js are seen simmering in the gloom

ABOVE A winter scene in the disused longshed at Suijatun running shed, Shenyang

Sankong Bridge, China – The Greatest Train-Watching Place in the World

OCCIDOR, THE CHINA TRAVEL specialists, commissioned me to lead a number of groups during the 1980s and early 1990s. We devised an excellent itinerary that centred around the busy main lines of Manchuria but also included Anshan Iron and Steel Works, the big open-cast pit at Manzholi, close to the Russian border, Nancha Bank on the line northwards to Yichun and, during the 1980s, the building of QJ and JS Classes at Datong.

There were also some extra-curricular attractions like the Forbidden City, Tienamen Square, The Great Wall and, in winter, the wonderful Harbin Ice Festival in Zhaolin Park. All of these tours were extremely successful, not least because of the excellent support given by the Chinese travel services.

One of the highlights of these expeditions was Sankong Bridge in Harbin which I dubbed in the itinerary as 'The greatest train-watching place in the world'. The bridge overlooks the vast marshalling yards where the southbound trains were assembled. It was a modest structure with three arches but a peep over the parapet rolled back the clock 50 years. Twelve steam locomotives might be visible in a sea of wagons that stretched as far as the eye could see. Harbin was an important junction for lines radiating to China's far northeast. It was a hump yard with wagons of many different types carrying every conceivable type of merchandise rolling singly or in groups through King and Queen points before crossing primary and secondary retarders. These actions were accompanied by the amplified voice of the yard controller who directed all the operations.

Until the late 1980s shunting was done by American-style JF Mikados. Their activities, interspersed with light engines coming to and from the shed, along with transfer freights and through freights, provided constant action. However, the best moments were the majestic departure of the made-up trains behind two QJs or a QJ and a JS as they passed beneath the bridge to begin the steep climb up to Wang Gang. There were also great moments when the JF drew a 2,500-tonne rake out of the yard prior to humping. Slipping and occasionally stalling, the engine would struggle towards us with tortured exhaust beats that struck the underside of the bridge causing it to shake in an alarming manner. On busy days it is no exaggeration to say that a steam locomotive passed beneath the bridge every three minutes throughout the entire day. Even back in the 1980s I concluded that no other steam location on Earth saw more action.

In the summer Sankong Bridge was a delightful place, but in winter the biting Manchurian wind blew across the yard from the north in vicious, stinging blasts and temperatures dropped to as low as -30 degrees Centigrade on the coldest days. During winter totally different pictures could be made by going down into the yard and focusing on the fronts of the trains waiting to depart. On departure the exhaust and steam from the cylinder cocks was so dense in the low temperatures that the background was completely obliterated, leaving the sunlit front of the engine shrouded in swirling steam.

Sankong Bridge was a place of endless interest and I visited it on many occasions over successive expeditions to China. In total I spent the equivalent of seven full working days there recording its infinite variety of moods and variations.

ABOVE LEFT A brace of China Railways' QJ Class 2-10-2s double head a southbound freight bound for the marshalling yards at Harbin. The leading engine is blowing down and the train engine is about to do the same, unusual in this populated environment

ABOVE The JF Class Mikado 2-8-2 was the traditional heavy hump-shunting type at Sankong yard until replaced by diesels in the late 1980s

LEFT Two QJs head a southbound mixed freight out of Harbin's marshalling yards. Wood from the far northeast was a principal commodity carried on the busy steam main line through Manchuria from Harbin to Changchun and Shenyang

Shrouded in smoke and steam
this KD6 Class is the Chinese
version of America's classic S160
war engine of which over 2, 000
were built

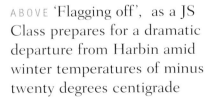

ABOVE 'Flagging off', as a JS Class prepares for a dramatic departure from Harbin amid winter temperatures of minus twenty degrees centigrade

RIGHT A pair of QJ Class 2-10-2s get a heavy southbound freight on the move from Harbin

193

The Gold Coast

VAST TRACTS OF FEVER-LADEN JUNGLE had to be penetrated by British engineers to construct the Gold Coast's first railway. The first locomotives were delivered in parts, landed by lighters and assembled on beaches with the help of native labour before being driven into the interior as the railway advanced. The railway works at Location were like the Black Country grafted onto primeval forest. All the machinery came from once-proud British companies that included Somerskill Brothers of Sowerby Bridge, Greenwood and Batley of Leeds and Joshua Bigwood. Clocks from Gents of Leicester, open-hearth furnaces from Alldays and Onions of Birmingham and hammers and anvils from Brooks of Lye. Almost the entire infrastructure was built in Britain.

The Gold Coast Railway was to become the pride of Africa. The network opened up huge industries including the Ashanti goldfields, cocoa to found the Cadbury empire, manganese, bauxite and timber. Passenger travel was luxurious and within two decades of the country being opened up, many trains were carrying restaurant cars and sleeping facilities. Travellers could assuage their thirsts with a bottle of Bass for 6d or a whisky and soda for 9d.

Once British control ceased following independence, Ghana Railways, in common with so many other British-operated railways around the world, began a marked decline. Even so, when I arrived in Accra in May 1985 I was shocked by the appalling state of the system. Few trains were running and no steam locomotives remained in operation. Many officials were frustrated by this, engines that Ghana had paid for and were simple to maintain, were preferable to diesels with all their attendant complications. 'More people walk on our railway than ever are carried by it,' I was told. The railway's inability to move products and materials in sufficient quantities was crippling many industries.

Quite apart from the operating tragedy, I sensed no will whatsoever to preserve any aspect of what was a dynamic Anglo-Ghanaian heritage. Stations, architecture, rolling stock, machine tools and locomotives were simply consigned to the past and considered irrelevant. The government was convening a huge conference on scrap disposal, a project that included much railway material and 3,300 tonnes of steam locomotives. All of which would pass conveniently to the steel works at Tema on the Atlantic coast.

At this time of great change in Ghana much could and should have been done to conserve something of the heritage. But even the responsible organisations in Britain have written Britain's railway legacy out of the history books. Yet if two nations were ever to work successfully together it would be Britain and Ghana. There was abundant evidence of a long colonial association with products like Milo, Bournvita, Ideal Milk and Omo being on ready sale. And in the row of shops alongside Accra's shed were 'Rita's Exciting Fashions' and 'Same Day Watch Works'. Post boxes were red with Elizabeth II on them.

Ghana's steam roster embraced seven different builders between 1921 and 1951. Many different types were evident but the bedrock of the fleet was the 4-8-2, a type first introduced to the Gold Coast by Nasmyth Wilson of Patricroft, Manchester in 1924. Many locomotives carried names commemorating local tribes, British governors, castles and even slaving ports like the vile Elmina Castle from where slaves were shipped to the New World in the 18th century. Jazz music developed as a result of the subsequent fusion of different races and I saw individuals in Ghana who resembled well-known jazz figures, the most dramatic being a lady in a market who looked exactly like Bessie Smith.

A scene in Accra, the Ghanaian capital, showing marketers who have moved in large numbers, and quite illegally, onto the disused sections of the depot yard. In the background on the left is a Hunslet 0-8-0T and to the right is a Vulcan Foundry 4-8-2

The cut-up pieces of a Nasmyth Wilson 4-8-2 No.123 'Prince of Wales' that was broken up within the depot confines at Kumasi

A study of Vulcan Foundry 130 Class 4-8-2 'E. M. Bland' at Kumasi on Tuesday 18th June 1985. The missing boiler had been sold to a local sawmill

Nameplates of condemned locomotives in the stores at Location. These commemorate tribes, former British governors of the Gold Coast and the slaving fort at Elmina Castle. I was reminded of nameplates in the stores at Crewe Works after the withdrawals of British steam during the 1960s. Tuesday 25th June 1985

RIGHT Abandoned 4-8-2 at Location Works. A picture that emphasises the highly characteristic British appearance of the Gold Coast's locomotives

LEFT Dated Friday 21st June 1985, this picture shows the boiler of a MacArthur 2-8-2 War Engine. It was discovered at the BLLC Sawmill in Kumasi. The meter-gauge MacArthurs were important engines during World War Two. At the end of hostilities dispersals were made to many parts of the world including the Gold Coast

BELOW A builder's plate from the MacArthur at BLLC Sawmill

FAR LEFT The forge at Location Works, complete with an anvil from Brooks of Lye. Monday 24th June 1985

LEFT 'The old forger', Location Works. Tuesday 25th June 1985

The Sudan

BRITAIN'S RAILWAY INTERESTS in the Sudan gave rise to one of Africa's finest railway systems whose main line was almost 1,400 miles long extending from Wadi Halfa on the Egyptian border to Wau in the far south. My arrival in Khartoum just before Christmas 1982, was the beginning of a highly successful expedition.

I was allocated an inspection saloon to tour the system that was attached to service trains as required so enabling a significant part of the system to be visited. My guide from the Ministry of Culture was Mustafa Karrar and our attendant/cook was a warm-hearted Nubian named Hussin. The saloon consisted of a lounge/dining room, double bedroom, bathroom, attendant's sleeping quarters and a kitchen. It was carpeted throughout and had space for bicycles for us to use on short-haul journeys when we camped at various centres.

Boxing day was spent shopping for supplies in Khartoum before our vehicle was attached to a northbound empty stock train bound for Atbara, one of the world's greatest railway towns. The 210-mile journey took 12 hours and on arrival we transferred to the railway guest house. Lunch was served with Sheffield cutlery on Staffordshire crockery marked 'Sudan Railways'. The coffee pots were Sheffield plate from Mappin & Webb and Heinz ketchup completed the scene.

Every nut and bolt of that massive works had come from Britain, even the works manager had been trained at Doncaster in the early 60s. It was deeply disturbing to see how the pride and magnificence of this once superb railway system had been dissipated. Many engines had been cannibalised for spares. The railway had been forced to apply tariffs to keep prices low and exports cheap. Sometimes the government ordered goods to be carried free and a lack of foreign exchange prevented the purchase of essential spares for locomotives and rolling stock. The parts they desperately needed at Atbara were simple items in terms of British technology; steel tyres, injectors, tubes, superheaters, firebox and tube plates.

Saudi Arabia and Germany had given large sums of money to Sudan for road-building so trucks and cars have flooded the country and in doing so have weakened the railway even further. The works contained many designs, including North British-built Pacifics and Mikados and the works pilot was a Hunslet 0-6-0T of 1950, one of the last main-line steam shunting engines ever built.

After a week in Atbara, the saloon was attached to a southbound passenger train. The destination this time was Sennar Junction, the best steam centre in the Sudan. On the way we stopped to visit the Gezira Project at Wad Medani. This was the biggest cotton project in the world and had an incredible network of over 800 miles of 600mm-gauge track. I was convinced that some steam locomotives might be found on the system but I was to be disappointed and after several days we continued to Sennar Junction.

The depot at Sennar Junction had an allocation of seven Pacifics and three Mikados. Life here was pleasant and apart from the railway delights, large flocks of Yellow Wagtails were present. These were Europe's wintering birds attracted by the presence of the nearby Sennar Dam. After a six-day stay in sidings next to the loco shed, the saloon was attached to the twice-weekly passenger train to El Damazeen close to the Ethiopian border. The ten-coach train was hauled through the golden desert by one of Sennar's blue Pacifics complete with an LNER-type squeaky whistle.

The priority at El Damazeen was to see the Clayton steam railcar that was dumped there. It was magnificent and almost identical to the 11 examples Clayton built for the LNER and named after famous stagecoaches such as 'Chevvy Chase', 'Bang Up', 'Comet' and 'Rapid'. Although outwardly complete, the railcar's vertical boiler and valve gear were missing.

After returning to Sennar we continued our southbound journey down the main line to Kosti. We were travelling for two days, the country becoming increasingly wild as massive termite mounds appeared on the tracksides and camels roamed freely in a golden landscape studded with baobab trees.

Kosti is an important trans-shipment point between the railway and the Nile for goods going to Malakal and Juba in the deep south. The railway also continues westwards from Kosti to Nyala and Wau. Nyala was soon to become the centre of world attention following the severe famines that were affecting those living in the Darfur region.

Kosti was the home of the huge 500 Class 4-8-2s, 42 of which were built for Sudan Railways by the North British in 1955. It was symptomatic of the entire network that only two of these remained in traffic. The other 40 lay idle needing spares.

On returning to Khartoum our saloon was stabled in the goods yard and I took the opportunity to photograph one of the Nile dredging vessels, a magnificent Scottish-built paddle steamer named 'Agrab'. She was built by W. M. Simons & Company Limited, Engineers and Shipbuilders of Renfrew No.495. She was up from the deep south for repairs.

While in Khartoum I also had meetings with the General Manager of Sudan Railways and the Minister of Transport. I had learned much on the tour and had seen once again the tragedy that can so easily befall a once great railway. They asked for help and for a greater liaison with Britain. I believe there should be an on-going relationship between Britain and the railways she once built and operated. And not just from an operational viewpoint but also with the aim of preserving key aspects of the joint heritage. I promised to give every publicity to the situation on Sudan Railways and in terms of preservation, a list of potential artefacts was drawn up.

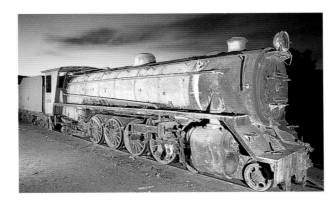

LEFT Sudan Railways' 500 Class 4-8-2 No.504 lies out of use at Kosti on Thursday 20th January 1983

BELOW Sunset at Khartoum invokes typical British aspects, the illuminated mosque is no longer incongruous. January 1983

TOP LEFT Sudan Railways' 500 Class 4-8-2 peeps out of the shed into the afternoon sunshine at Kosti and receives attention from the fitters. Tuesday 25th January 1983

LEFT Sennar Junction Depot with Sudan Railways' Pacific No.246 (left) and Mikado No.316 (right). Sunday 9th January 1983

ABOVE A Sudan Railways' 500 Class 4-8-2 slips vigorously on greasy rails

TOP RIGHT Receiving a fitter's attention at Sennar Junction

RIGHT Alldays & Onions openhearth furnace with ladle and anvil at Kosti Motive Power Depot. Tuesday 25th January 1983

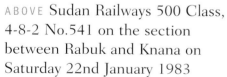 Sudan Railways 500 Class, 4-8-2 No.541 on the section between Rabuk and Knana on Saturday 22nd January 1983

TOP RIGHT Sudan Railways 500 Class, 4-8-2 No.541 on the Rabuk to Knana line passing the wreck of sister engine No.514

RIGHT A track trolley built by Wickham of Ware reposes at Singa as a Sennar to Damazeen freight departs. Monday 17th January 1983

Britain's Last Exported Steam Locomotive, Java

IN THE COMPOSITION CALLED 'Rice Boy', we see a diminutive tank engine collecting sugar cane from a Javan village surrounded by rice paddies. The boy's name is Iswanto and the village is Karanglegi Lor, located in the Trangkil Sugar Mill plantation near Pati in central Java. Iswanto was 13 when he was caught resting on the bank of the rice paddy in July 1989. How could one explain to him the significance of the fussy little saddle tank that daily collected cane from the siding near his home. To him it was commonplace; every village had one.

However, that diminutive tank engine was far from commonplace, it had a unique place in the history of the industrial revolution – it was the last steam locomotive exported from Britain. The last of tens of thousands built in foundries whose names are enshrined in industrial folklore. The engines were rolled onto the decks of ships for export to all parts of the world in the name of Britain's industrial revolution.

Britain began exporting steam locomotives in the 1830s and continued to do so until the 1970s, almost one and a half centuries later, and the tradition ended when this little 0-4-2ST left Hunslet's works in Leeds in 1971 as their works No.3902. I was reminded that once there were five locomotive builders in the Leeds parish of Hunslet and all were involved in the overseas market.

When built, the little Hunslet went to the Indonesian Forestry Commission but was transferred to Trangkil in 1974. So far as I am aware it was the only British-built locomotive in service on the Javan sugar plantations. Despite the island having hundreds of different locomotives of many different designs, almost all were of Dutch or German origin. As an example, Trangkil had four steam locomotives, all of different design and from three different countries.

Trangkil's 0-4-2ST was actually a Kerr Stuart 'Brazil' Class, Hunslet having acquired the goodwill of this Stoke on Trent builder when they ceased trading in the 1930s. Consequently there was a considerable number of parts for the Brazil type in stock at Hunslet when the order from Java came through.

The engine had slide valves and, when working, emitted the wet, throaty coughs characteristic of such engines. Lighting on the little Hunslet was by Stone of Deptford, lubrication by British Detroit and injectors by Gresham Craven of Manchester.

Over 350 organisations are known to have built steam locomotives in Britain and the building perspective is interesting. The first was built in 1803 and the last example for main-line service was built in 1960.

Four more years were to elapse before the last one was built for the National Coal Board and this was regarded as definitively the last. And then, seven years later, the long-obsolete Kerr Stuart 'Brazil' type suddenly came back to life.

ABOVE Builder's plate

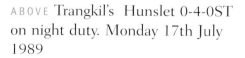

ABOVE Trangkil's Hunslet 0-4-0ST
on night duty. Monday 17th July
1989

TOP RIGHT Trangkil's Hunslet
0-4-0ST at Karanglegi Lor
loading sidings on Thursday
20th July 1989

RIGHT 'Rice Boy' is 13-year-old
Iswanto and each day the little
Hunslet comes to the local
sidings next to his village to
collect cane. The engine's Baguley
Price valve gear is clearly visible.
Wednesday 19th July 1989

Java Sugar Fields

NO AREA OF THE WORLD has a greater diversity of colourful steam locomotives than the sugar plantations of Java. Sadly, what was once a veritable treasure-trove is now much diminished. A decline in the industry has seen a reduction in the amount of active mills and the incidence of trucking has become another factor. But even today, many of the locomotives remain extant and along with China, Java remains an irresistible attraction and if one's interest is in narrow-gauge systems, there is nowhere on Earth that compares with Java.

The motive power consists principally of tender tank engines comprised of 0-4-0, 0-4-2, 0-6-0, 0-8-0 and 0-10-0 along with 0-4-4-0 Mallets. Innumerable different designs and liveries occur. Most of the engines are of German manufacture between 1900 and 1920, the year when the industry was being developed under Dutch rule. The 700mm gauge clearly dominates but some factories were laid to 600mm.

Almost all engines burn bagasse, the natural waste product of sugar-cane processing, and although its calorific value is low it means that the locomotives run on fuel which is free. Java is famous for its volcanoes and it is a delightful practice to name many of the locomotives after these, often with attractive rectangular nameplates cast in brass with raised letters on a red background.

The following extract from my diary reveals the activities at Pesantren Mill in east Java with its yellow liveried locomotives: 'Between the hours of 22.00 and midnight I went to the yards hoping to see some action. No trains were in when I arrived, the only engine being 'Wilis', a 1901-built 0-4-2T from Arnold Jung. She was on yard duty pushing the rakes of cane up to the factory crushers. Soon a heavy main liner arrived behind 'Semeru', an 0-6-0TT by Orenstein and Koppel in 1920 that was named after Java's highest volcano. She got a clear road into the sidings and her heavy wagons rumbled past piled precariously high with cane. Within minutes the operators cabin was offered another train from a different line and so arrived an Orenstein and Koppel 1925-built 0-8-0TT, delightfully named 'Penanggungan' after a large mountain. It followed 'Semeru' into the yard. With two full trains in 'Wilis' was busy assembling the rakes as the tender engines, having gone to the shed, took water and bagasse before returning to the plantation. By 11.15, a third freight was offered but this was held outside the factory to allow 'Semeru's' departure with empties and with an enormous rake chattering and bowling along behind her, she raised the echoes and thundered away into the night. Afterwards, a heavy coughing exhaust became audible interspersed by some vigorous slipping; with steam hissing from her cylinder cocks the labouring engine crawled forwards. It was 'Dieng' an Orenstein and Koppel 0-8-0TT of 1922. Her name commemorated the famous plateau in central Java. 'Dieng' was checked again at the factory entrance and stood hissing impatiently until a road was prepared amid the general yard activity; a busy night indeed.'

An Orenstein and Koppel builder's plate from an 0-4-2T at Sragi Sugar Mill

ABOVE 'Rice Girl' at Karanglegi Lor was 11-year-old Jamini

LEFT The crew of 'Badang', a Vulcan Ironworks 0-6-0TT of 1920, take a break in the plantation at Jatiwangi Sugar Mill. Friday 7th July 1989

TOP LEFT Jatiwangi Sugar Mill No.5 'Banteng' (Rhinoceros), an Orenstein and Koppel 0-8-0T of 1912 at one of the system's loading sidings

TOP RIGHT Pagottan Mill's No.7, an Orenstein and Koppel 0-10-0TT of 1926, on Thursday 3rd August 1989

LEFT 'Guntur', an Orenstein and Koppel 0-8-0T of 1913, with Klein Linder axles at Purwodadi Sugar Mill, Madiun, on 31st August 1989

FAR LEFT 'The Sandman' whose job was to spray the tracks ahead of the locomotive to prevent slipping when the tracks were wet or greasy. A scene at Meritjan Sugar Mill, Kediri, with a Borsig 0-8-0TT of 1912

LEFT The vibrant colours of Java's sugar-mill locomotives combine with their constant fiery effects to provide tremendous photographic excitement

BELOW 'Bringing in the cane by night.' Left, an 0-4-4-0, 700mm-gauge, four-cylinder compound Mallet from the Dutch builder Ducroo and Brauns in 1928. Right, No.8, 'Dieng' an Orenstein and Koppel 0-8-0TT of 1922 with Klein Linder axles at Pesantren Sugar Mill, Kediri, on Thursday 27th July 1989. This picture was a re-make of a theme from the 1974 expedition

The Legendary 'El Esla'

AS LATE AS THE 1970s Spain had a remarkable variety of ancient locomotives active in industrial environments and centenarians were not uncommon. By the mid eighties most had disappeared with the notable exception of 'El Esla', a beautiful Sharp Stewart 0-6-0T, built at their Great Bridgewater Street works, Manchester in 1885 as works number 3343. She survived at Sabero colliery and during the scripting for Nick Dodson's Railfilms video 'Around the World in Search of Steam' that was a profile of my work, we decided to include 'El Esla'.

We spent three days filming at Sabero in May 1987 and one of the comments I had to say to camera as I stood alongside 'El Esla' was 'when this engine left Sharp, Stewart's Great Bridgewater Street works in Manchester bound for Spain, Queen Victoria had another 16 years to rule the British Empire'. The engine, 102 years old at that time, exuded 19th century vintage and was a typical Sharp Stewart design.

One of the sequences in the video depicts the photography of 'El Esla' as she emerged from the tunnel between the colliery and exchange sidings. With my camera tightly focused on the tunnel and the hillside above and the sun shining directly into the tunnel mouth, I waited until the engine's beautiful shape emerged from the darkness.

Then as the smoke gathered around, haloing the engine against the black interior, I let the exhaust shoot out of the tunnel before firing the camera. We were able to arrange a number of run-outs to select exactly the right steam-billowing effect, each take being subtly different from the previous one.

Notice also that 'El Esla' was a Sharp Stewart Manchester engine that was built two years before the company moved to Glasgow. Sharp Stewart continued to build in Glasgow until 1903 when, in the light of increasing competition from America, they merged with Dubs and Neilson, the other two leading Glasgow builders, to form the mighty North British, the largest locomotive builder in Europe.

ABOVE Still life: detail from 'El Esla's footplate

LEFT 'El Esla' emerges from the coal screen at Sabero Colliery

The Ghost of Olloniego

THE IBERIAN EXPEDITION OF APRIL 1971 was by motor caravan; there were five of us. It was a railway tour but one member, Duncan McNeal, was an ornithologist with more than a passing interest in railways. The early days of the month saw us at Alsasua for the massive Spanish National Railways' 4-8-4 Confederation and by the 5th we had reached Meires Colliery with its vintage British engines of the 1870s and 1880s. But the morning of the 6th provided an even greater revelation when we arrived at Olloniego Colliery in the pouring rain with a leaden grey sky. For there, dragging itself around the colliery yard, was an apparition that looked as if it dated back to the dawn of the steam locomotive; a truly primeval beast in the shape of an 0-8-0 built in Germany by Hartmann in 1879 complete with Stephenson valve gear. She was numbered 2151 and formally named 'El Cavado' after the Spanish river and was an ex-Norte Railway mainline freight hauler. The basic design dated back to the 1860s and must have been one of the first 0-8-0s ever built. The engine had a four-wheel tender that was quite out of proportion and had come from a condemned 0-6-0 of 1850s vintage.

Shrouded in steam and issuing anguished throaty coughs, the veteran propelled a long rake of wagons up the colliery yard but the inclement weather rendered photography virtually impossible and anyway within an hour of our arrival, the engine had broken a tender spring and was set aside for on-the-spot repairs. I couldn't believe our luck in finding such a locomotive and I automatically assumed that we would wait a day at Olloniego for the spring to be repaired and the weather to improve. Not at all, my companions were not prepared to lose a day for one engine. They were keen to move on to the varied delights of Portugal. There was no choice but to go along with their decision and with heavy heart I left the veteran simmering in the pouring rain with its tender jacked up.

I never forgot that engine but in the cut and thrust of world expeditions never managed to get back to Olloniego. The years passed and I reasoned that the engine, in an advanced state of decrepitude when I found it, almost certainly would have been set aside and broken up. The dreams turned to legend and I used to tell the story of this amazing 0-8-0 I found in Spain many years ago.

Then came the script for Nick Dodson's video on my work, 'Around the World in Search of Steam' and our decision to include in the film 'El Esla', a vintage meter-gauge Sharp Stewart 0-6-0T that survived at Sabero Colliery. Why not include Olloniego? I imagined telling the story to camera in the partly regenerated site of the long-since-closed old coalmine.

Almost 16 years later, in mid May 1987, I approached Olloniego village once more. There, up on high ground stood the colliery, its rail connection long since severed. A high-sided lorry parked in the middle of loading hoppers indicated some on-going production. I scanned the yard for any signs of railway equipment but nothing was evident. Although this was what I had expected, I still felt a surge of disappointment. A closer inspection of the yard was made but clearly there was nothing. Dejectedly, I climbed to the top of a high bank of colliery waste that gave a good view of the entire yard through to the loading hoppers. A patch of orange among the overgrown buildings caught my eye, my pulse began to race as I interpreted its contours into a locomotive. Involuntarily I let out a shout and ran down the colliery yard. Clad in a blaze of vivid rust the 108-year-old survivor looked even more exciting than before. I clambered through the branches and into the cab; climbed along the boiler and peered down the chimney that had almost rusted through where it joined the smokebox. It was a miracle that the engine had survived; the colliery yard having been stripped of all infrastructure including rails. There was clearly no intention of preservation as the engine had been left to rot.

How providence conspired to reunite me with that engine I will never know, any more than I know its fate, but I am proud to have captured it for posterity, for neither the ghost of Olloniego nor anything like it, will ever be seen again.

An engine to dream on. The
Hartmann 0-8-0 of 1879,
complete with Stephenson valve
gear, as re-discovered on the
expedition in May 1987. The
ghost-like quality of these pictures
resemble an ocean-floor theme

TOP Detail of the Hartmann 0-8-0
with previous year's bird's nest

BOTTOM Safety-valve detail of the
Hartmann 0-8-0

TOP Splasher detail of the
Hartmann 0-8-0

BOTTOM Cylinder detail of the
Hartmann 0-8-0

Cuba – Last Bastion of Classic American Steam

THE TROPICAL ISLAND OF CUBA is a treasure house of classic American steam frozen in time by Fidel Castro's 1959 revolution. America inherited Cuba following the Spanish-American war and effectively the island became a colony, such industry as was developed being American.

Fidel Castro ousted the puppet dictator Batista and that led to America imposing sanctions on Cuba that remain in place to this day.

In terms of technology, Cuba became a place that time forgot. The American railroad equipment was never updated and remained active in Cuba long after it had been replaced elsewhere. Few of Cuba's locomotives are more recent than the 1920s. Some date back to the 1870s and Cuba has more centenarian steam locomotives than anywhere else on Earth.

Although steam has disappeared from the island's state network, it survives in some variety on the railways of the sugar mills – sugar lies at the heart of Cuba's economy.

All locomotives are oil burners, the island having no indigenous reserves of coal. The hauls from the plantation to the mills could be lengthy and the heavily loaded trains frequently ran over the metals of the main-line network. Sonorous whippoorwill whistles, clanging bells and wooden signal boxes on stilts are all elements evocative of American practice. Dozens of different designs with delightfully varied liveries operated over a variety of gauges: Consolidations, Pacifics, Prairies, Mikados, 2-4-0s and 0-4-0STs embracing many historic builders.

The seasonal nature of the sugar milling has done much to keep the vintage steam running, there being ample time both for maintenance and a general make-do-and-mend culture as the locomotives are active only during the milling campaign.

Cuba's great historical claim to fame is, of course, its Havana cigars that have been revered worldwide for centuries and during my expedition to the island in March and April 1988, I spent a fascinating week in the Vuelta Abajo region where the finest leaves are grown. I was able to see at first hand the growing, harvesting and curing processes and to sample some field varieties of cigars that were superb and totally different from well-known brands. In Havana I spent a day at the La Corona factory where I saw women and girls hand rolling cigars, though sadly not on their thighs!

Cuba's cigars, glorious climate, rolling blue ocean, golden beaches and the happy welcoming faces of its people, laced with classic American steam make for a heady mix.

Sadly, the early years of the 20th century saw a dramatic decline in Cuba's sugar industry; many mills closed or reduced production making dieselisation easier on the those that survived. Although the diversity of locomotives remained in situ, most are no longer active.

Even the legendary Havanas are not what they used to be. Inconsistencies, especially in the rolling, have enabled other countries such as the Dominican Republic and Honduras, to compete and although Cuban cigars are still the best, Britain's 'Daily Telegraph' has reported a shift in the nation's boardrooms to brands other than Havanas.

FAR LET Robles flat crossing with signal box on stilts at Boris Luis Santa Coloma Sugar Mill with Baldwin Mogul, Works No.53822 approaching

LEFT A scene on the 2ft 7½in-gauge system of Simon Bolivar, Sancti Spiritus Province.

BOTTOM LEFT Venceremos (We shall overcome) on a Baldwin 2-8-0 at Boris Luis Santa Coloma Sugar Mill. Tuesday 12th April 1988

BOTTOM Baldwin 2-8-0 No.1390 heads a loaded train over the Arroyo Blanco line of the Rafael Freyre Sugar Mill in Holguin Province. Monday 18th April 1988

TOP RIGHT The most powerful
engines on Cuba are these 1900
Class 2-8-0s. Here is No.1907, a
Baldwin from 1924, at Carlos
Manuel de Cespedes Sugar Mill
in Camaguey Province. Tuesday
19th April 1988

ABOVE Baldwin 0-4-0F No.1170
of 1916 shunts amid the palms at
Bolivia Sugar Mill Camaguey
Province on Friday 22nd April
1988

RIGHT This superb green-liveried
Baldwin 2-8-0 of 1920 was caught
hauling a yellow caboose at
George Washington Sugar Mill in
Villa Clara Province on Monday
25th April 1988

LEFT Boiler explosion. The remains of 'Manuel Fajardo', a Baldwin 2-8-0 of 1916 that blew up at Obdulio Morales Sugar Mill in Sancti Spiritus Province. The driver, who was applying a round of oil to the engine's motion at the time of the explosion, was literally blown to pieces, only his legs were found

BELOW 'A tale of two Alcos' at the George Washington Sugar Mill in Villa Clara Province. On the left is Alco Schenectady 2-8-0 No.1730 of 1913 along with an Alco Brooks Works 0-6-0T of 1916. This engine, numbered 134, was part of the United Railways of Havana. Before the shoot, the 0-6-0's chimney was missing and had to be physically retrieved from a nearby house in which it was being used as a flower pot – hence the difference in colour!

The Broad-Gauge Discovery, Azores

FOR YEARS RUMOURS EXISTED about there being two seven-foot-gauge locomotives at Ponta del Garda in the Azores. Surely the Azores, those tiny mid-Atlantic islands, never had a railway. And assuming they did, they would hardly be seven-foot gauge. It was a popular belief that following the abolition of Brunel's broad gauge in 1892, all conventional seven-foot gauge locomotives had been broken up by 1900.

But the concept still haunted me and I commissioned a Portuguese interpreter to come to Newton Harcourt and sit by the phone until the matter had been resolved. It took several hours to make contact with the harbour at Ponta del Garda but we managed to speak to the harbour-master. Breathlessly I waited for his response. The interpreter turned and said, 'yes, there is a railway there but it has not been used in many years and only two locomotives remain'. 'And what is the gauge?' I asked. 'He doesn't know.' I grabbed the interpreters arm: 'Ask him to send someone out to measure the distance between the rails and we will call back in an hour'. I was in suspended animation with visions of Brunel's dream, an exotic expedition and the world's only broad-gauge locomotives.

It took another two hours for the call to come through. 'The harbourmaster has sent a runner to measure the rails but he cannot find them. They are buried in the soil.' My agonised reply was 'let him send another runner to dig out the rails and measure them'. We were asked to ring back at 14.00 the following afternoon. The next day we rang as arranged but the harbourmaster was not in the office and no one knew about our quest. 'Ring back at 16.00,' it was suggested. We did and spoke to the harbourmaster: 'The distance between the rails is 213cms,' he said.

Unbelievable, seven foot! The expedition was on.

One week later, on a damp, dark November morning, I left Newton Harcourt for Lisbon and from there to fly to the Azores. The following morning Alvaro Saraiva, my guide-to-be arrived at the hotel, and we got on extremely well. We drove to the old dock area at the far end of the harbour. It was now little more than a junk yard with derelict harbour machinery and old upturned boats.

'There they are,' Alvaro declared as he stopped the vehicle. I could see nothing until a rusty chimney top, protruding above a mess of debris, caught my attention.

Peering through the junk a whole new dimension of railways opened up and I could see the breathtaking beauty of a seven-foot gauge locomotive. The sheer monumentality of Brunel's vision made the standard gauge look like a toy. However, debris made photography impossible, and the second engine was completely covered.

I explained the difficulties to Alvaro who went to discuss the problem with the harbour authorities. He returned beaming, 'I have organised a crane, a heavy forklift truck, a lorry and six men to clear the site'. We worked feverishly that afternoon and the next day by which time the second engine stood clear. I surveyed the two giants and became aware of the irony of having travelled thousands of miles to these semi-tropical islands only to find that the first locomotive was from the Falcon Works at Loughborough in Leicestershire, just 20 miles from Newton Harcourt!

The second locomotive to be uncovered was a Black Hawthorn from Gateshead built in 1883.

We did a superb job of clearing the site but the engines had been pushed together buffer to buffer, not ideal for photography.

'Leave it to me,' Alvaro said and leaving me to dig out the rails from under the soil, he disappeared only to return two hours later riding atop the most hideous pneumatic forklift truck and beaming all over his face. Lashings of steel coil were applied to the Falcon's frame and the forklift, revved to screaming pitch, was flung into gear. In a violent cataclysm of movement it lurched the locomotive forward very slightly.

The local media arrived, Azores TV and a journalist from the local paper. No one had any knowledge of the engine's significance, neither had they heard of Brunel. Many onlookers also thought it incredulous that I should have come so far to see two scrap engines that didn't even work. By this time we were preparing the locomotives for photography and I gave Alvaro the task of putting a coat of paint on the engine's running plate and connecting rods. This caused more incredulity from those watching, painting a rusty engine and putting the paint on top of the rust was incomprehensible to them.

The locomotives were so derelict that they couldn't be painted easily and the result was gaudy and needed to be toned down. The preferred method was to throw handfuls of dust and soil at the fresh paint to provide the necessary faded look. The crowd were delighted by this and by now they were convinced that I was a complete eccentric.

Perfection was but a hair's breath away but we had to do something about the huge white wall that stood behind the engines. 'What can we come up with?' I asked. 'How about some branches?' 'There are no trees on the coastline, only in the interior of the island' Alvares said.

Next morning a pick-up truck arrived at the hotel and we set off inland to find some conifers. When we got back to the harbour the trees were put into a large heap next to the Falcon.

Assembly was daunting. There was nothing to stick the trees into and they were as heavy as mahogany. We laboured long and hard and covered the wall effectively having attempted to lash the trees together with wire.

However, before any photography could begin, the sky darkened, the wind rose, a squally mid-Atlantic storm was welling up. The ferocious gusts of wind set about the conifers with relish. They swayed alarmingly for a few minutes before they went down like a row of ninepins. Some of the smallest even blew away up the harbour. Alvaro looked at me as if he wished I would go home.

Having completed the photography I was received by the Governor of the Azores to put the case for the preservation of the engines and the possible repatriation of one to Britain. He assured me that everyone in the Azores now knew the significance of the relics and that they would not be broken up.

Back in England there was widespread national publicity for our discovery; an interview on BBC Radio 4's 'Today' programme was broadcast, there was a full-colour page in the 'Illustrated London News' and four pages in 'Steam Railway Magazine' when Mike George was the editor. And now, 25 years later, it seems that both engines are destined to remain in the Azores.

ABOVE The Black Hawthorn Saddle Tank lashed by a squally mid-Atlantic storm. The width of the buffer beam reflects the seven-foot gauge

LEFT The harbour breakwater at Ponta del Garda showing the cast concrete tetrapodos that have replaced the traditional boulders. Saturday 7th November 1981

BELOW The world's last two conventional broad-gauge locomotives, the Falcon is on the right and the Black Hawthorn is to the rear. This picture shows the cleared site with the conifers securely set in position

Building the World's Last Steam Locomotives, SYs at Tangshan

TANGSHAN WORKS HAD A nineteenth century atmosphere and was building some eighty SYs a year. The rough castings shop was like a scene from the 1850s. The workers moved across the earth floor filling the moulds with sand as the sunlight streamed in through blackened windows. A wagon bearing a huge ladle of liquid steel was periodically winched along an intershop trackway. The overhead crane picked up the ladle and flitted it across the shop floor, visiting every mould with its fertilising touch, like a bee moving from bloom to bloom.

In the adjacent shop, mounds of dull grey castings were heaped up amid the gloom; wheels, cylinders, frame sections being immediately recognisable. The deafening blast of heavy drilling indicated that the rough castings were being produced in readiness for subsequent machining. Periodically the ground would tremble as an explosion shook the entire shop - a hot cylinder casting had been dropped into water thence to be carried by the overhead crane, still steaming, to join the castings waiting to go to the machining and finishing shops.

In the forges, blackened men flitted amid the gloom and the ground shook with the thumps of steam hammers of many sizes pounding the red hot ingots into shape. In the centre stood one of gargantuan proportions performing its hypnotic task and exploiting the malleability of a white hot Anshan billet which it gradually elongated and shaped to form the driving axle of an SY locomotive.

Each stroke caused the earth to tremble and I thought of the mighty hammer that James Naysmyth had supplied to the Woolwich Arsenal, the blows from which could clearly be felt from the Greenwich Observatory two miles away.

In an adjacent shop, I came upon three men manufacturing firebox rivets. One man drew the pieces of red hot metal from the furnace and placed them in a machine driven by a rapidly revolving flywheel. The rivets were punched into shape before the machine flung them, still glowing, into a carefully placed wheel barrow - never missing! The wheel barrow stood bathed in shafts of smoky sunlight that seeped into the forge.

In the boiler shop, the inner and outer sections of fireboxes were riveted before moving forward to receive the barrel sections which were being welded together. As the boiler progressed along the shop, the tube plates were fitted, followed by the tubes themselves. Next came the superheater elements followed by the hydraulic test.

Simultaneously, the boiler received its flamingo orange undercoat and was then ready for placing on to an internal rail wagon for transfer to the erecting shop. During my stay, I watched an SY grow from the frame stage to the fitting of cylinders and lowering of the boiler after which the cab was swung into place. A swarm of workers then descended to complete the fitting up and the entire engine turned into a mass of welders flashes as the overhead cranes flitted back and forth bringing all manner of small parts.

Welding, bolting or drilling, the men worked rapidly; they knew every action, every screw, every joint and weld. But the most dramatic moment was to come when a set of wheels arrived from the finishing shop and when these had been placed in the Mikado formation the two overhead cranes combined to lift the locomotive to enable the shining red wheels to be rolled beneath. The stately momentum of this operation was every bit as magnificent as the ceremonial launching of a great ship. The flamingo liveried SY is then drawn out of the erecting shop by the works pilot, a scruffy YJ 2-6-2, and the new-born joins her tender. The complete locomotive is now drawn over to the steam testing shop.

Entering this building was a spine tingling experience for within its darkened portals the giants received their first breath of animation to stand under steam through twenty four hours, with a dozen blue overalled fitters attending to detailed adjustments.

Soon the new-born is moving around the works yard under her own power ready for a test run on the main line and she will run at full throttle for the twelve and a half mile stretch to Tienzhuang. After proving, the SYs returned to the works to enter the paint shop before their rods are taken down and they are placed in the work's sidings in readiness to be conveyed to their destination by freight train. Within hours they disappeared, so great was China's need for industrial locomotives.

TOP LEFT The boiler shop at
Tangshan Works

TOP RIGHT Newly built SY Class
2-8-2 No.1722 in works orange
undercoat, is lowered on to its
wheels. Picture taken from the
overhead crane at Tangshan
Works on New Year's Day 1992.
The characters on the crane read;
" The worker's dicipline needs to
be as hard as the iron"

BOTTOM LEFT A welder works on
detail parts at Tangshan

BOTTOM RIGHT The carbon
converter in demonic vein. To the
left is a former China Railway's
coach in use as a bothy

TOP LEFT Firebox riveting

BOTTOM LEFT Un-machined
wheels from sand moulds

RIGHT Steam hammer pounding a
red hot ingot

Eritrea, Rebirth of Steam

'Our railway system will serve as an historical monument.'
Ato Amanuel Ghebresilasie
Head of Eritean Railway Transport, October 1997

IN THE MID 1990s the newly formed African state of Eritrea rediscovered the age of steam and began to restore its 950mm-gauge former Italian colonial railway that operated between the 16th century port of Massawa on the Red Sea coast and Asmara, the capital.

This decision followed Eritrea becoming an independent nation in 1993 after 30 years of civil war with Ethiopia.

During the civil war the railway was looted, track was taken up for use in military bunkers and passenger stock utilised as army sleeping quarters. The decision to rebuild the railway was highly imaginative and easily caught the interest of the whole nation as a civil project that would benefit everyone.

But it was an awesome undertaking. Eritrea is one of the poorest nations on earth and the route forms one of the most tortuous mountain railways in the world. From Massawa, the line climbs 7,143 feet above sea level during its 74-mile ascent up the fog-shrouded Arborobu escarpment. 65 bridges and 30 tunnels are encountered on the way. Without the railway, the only communication between the docks at Massawa and the capital is by a treacherous narrow highway that is a death trap by any standards and the sight of heavy trucks lying in ravines along the route is nothing unusual.

It is almost true to say that the rebuilding of the railway was either done with bare hands or, at best, with hand tools. Very little in the way of modern machinery was available and the project was pioneered with an absolute minimum of foreign help. Most of the locomotives had never turned a wheel in 25 years and many of those who had run the railway had long since retired. Undeterred, the government brought them back, men in their 70s, 80s and even 90s re-kindled their latent skills and during my month-long visit to Eritrea in February/March of 1998, it was awe inspiring to see the whole system coming to life again.

At the locomotive sheds in Asmara, the machine shops were opened up, boilers were strung up in mighty sheerlegs for re-tubing and all the processes of heavy overhauling got under way. As the work progressed, the whole country became mobilised. Rails were brought back from the old battlefields and sleepers from the former trenches.

The motive power roster embraces 0-4-0WTs from Breda of Milan in the 1920s and 30s; four-cylinder compound 0-4-4-0T Mallets from Ansaldo in 1938 and two superb Art Deco Littorina diesel railcars, built by Fiat in 1936. Other equipment included two Russian lorries, modified to run on the railway and an even more remarkable track-inspection trolley built out of a classic Motoguzzi motorcycle from the 1930s, complete with gear change on the side of the petrol tank.

Having successfully opened the Asmara to Massawa section, thought has since been given to extending the system a further 117 miles through Keren and on to Agordat close to the border with Sudan.

On my visit to Eritea I was accompanied by Carol my partner, and my daughter Marie-Louise and was supported by David Wright, an ex-patriot who lived and worked in Eritrea and had a passionate interest in the country's well being. David knows the country and its people intimately and we were able to tour the system in detail and watch it come back to life. At that time, operations had already begun between Massawa and Mai Attal (Goat's Drink) and of course at the running sheds in Asmara where several engines may be in steam in the depot yard at one time.

The re-birth of Eritrea's railways is a story almost without precedent and is remarkable by any criteria but it is a little more easily understood when one considers the character, imagination and innovation of the Eritrean people. They are friendly, industrious and socially minded. The country has the potential to become a model African state. And there's also the famous saying, that everyone will tell you: 'No one visits Eritrea once'.

Memories of that tour include visiting the Den Den military graveyard outside Asmara where a vast array of hardware including third-class balcony coaches, was assembled. Watching the first firing up of newly overhauled Breda 0-4-0WT No.202 004, travelling up and down the Arborobu escarpment and visiting old stations with their typical Italian architecture was a real pleasure and a great experience. But the most exciting adventure took place on 12th March when I travelled with Mallet No.442.59 from Mai Attal to Digdigta (High Place). We had a short engineer's train and I was able to make pictures along the way, having been assured that that particular area had been cleared of land mines! Seeing that lovely Mallet in the golden afternoon light heading up the escarpment, was an absolute triumph.

One could only hope that the Eritrean story will inspire other developing nations who have also lost their railway to embark on similar enterprises.

The newly re-opened locomotive sheds at Asmara with Italian-built Breda 0-4-0WTs in various stages of overhaul

ABOVE Ansaldo 0-4-4-0, four cylinder compound Mallet No.59, built in 1938, with an engineer's train at Digdigta, 22 miles from Massawa on Thursday 12th March 1998.

RIGHT Four-cylinder compound Ansaldo Mallet No.59 with an engineer's train between Mai Attal and Digdigta

Recalled artisans at work rehabilitating a Breda Well Tank at Asmara

LEFT The boiler of an Italian built Breda 0-4-0WT being overhauled in the magnificent sheerlegs at Asmara locomotive running shed

Pulgaon to Arvi – India's Last Narrow-Gauge Country Railway

I NEGLECTED INDIA'S WIDE DIVERSITY of 2ft 6in-gauge lines in favour of concentrating on the broad gauge and in particular the X Series Standards of the 1920s. Since turning professional in 1969 and despite making eight expeditions to India, there was much I simply didn't manage to cover. So the ten days spent on the Pulgaon to Arvi line in February 1997 were especially valuable. The line was, by then, the last 2ft 6in-gauge steam operation in India and I concentrated on its status as a typical country railway.

The line was once part of the Great Indian Peninsula Railway. It left the main-line station at Pulgaon to thread its way 21 miles across remote cotton-growing countryside to Arvi. The seven intermediate stations at Sorta, Virul, Rhona Town, Dhanori, Pargothan, Pachegaon and Kubgaon, were little more than tin shacks in the middle of nowhere, most of the villages they served being some distance away.

Originally the line was built to convey cotton to the large Victorian mill in Pulgaon. I was fortunate to obtain accommodation in the mill's guest house that was situated in a walled area of the factory compound. The residence was typically British and had beautifully tended lawns and flower beds so reminiscent of those I had grown up with in England. The mill also had a superb steam hooter that went off at each shift, it could have been Bolton in 1895.

Sadly the line is parallel with a road that has frequent buses in operation. These are more reliable and frequent than the trains and many villagers use the train only if they are carrying heavy commodities. The motive power consisted of three ZP Class Pacifics, built by Nippon in Japan in 1954. Originally built for the Satpura lines, the ZPs were transferred to Pulgaon in 1976 and were among the handful of Pacifics that survived in passenger service anywhere in the world. Shortage of spares and coal made operations a nightmare but fortunately only one locomotive was needed to maintain the service. Dieselisation was scheduled by the summer of 1997.

Punctuality was the exception rather than the rule. Mechanical problems and poor-quality coal that turned to clinker and blocked up the firebox were just two reasons for poor timekeeping but matters certainly were not helped by the engine crew's tendency to stop for prolonged tea breaks at Pargothan no matter how late the train may have been running.

I loved the line's remoteness and charming little stations and happily could have spent weeks photographing it as a social railway. I was well aware that very few country railways like this still existed. The pictures would be a last expression of something that, a hundred years ago, was a common form of transport worldwide.

My favourite picture was made in the station forecourt at Pargothan where a water hydrant was located and village women would come from far around to fill their urns and pots. When train No.643 'Down' that departed from Pulgaon at 08.00 and reached Arvi at 10.20 arrived, usually there would be a group of women at the hydrant and it was possible to photograph them with the train in the ramshackle station behind.

Every day for a week I was in position for the arrival of No.643 'Down' and for six days of that week the perfect picture eluded me. On the first day too few women were present, on the following day there were too many, on the third day, the women were fine but the weather was cloudy, on the fourth day the train stopped at the wrong place in the station and the engine was not visible, on the fifth day there were no women at all and on the sixth day, the figures around the hydrant were not grouped well. But on the seventh day everything fell into place and the country atmosphere of the line was truly captured.

ABOVE The ultimate picture at Pargothan with village women at the water hydrant and train No. 643 'Down' in the station.

ABOVE Train No. 643 'Up' from Arvi to Pulgaon arrives at Pargothan behind 2ft 6in-gauge ZP Class Pacific No.2

LEFT Country railway. Sorta was the first station out of Pulgaon on the line to Arvi. Morning commuters wait for train No.643 'Down', due to depart Pulgaon at 08.00

India - The End of Steam

THE HARROWING RUN DOWN of steam in Britain was a time of great sadness and when the last fire was dropped in 1968 a million hearts were broken, we never thought it would happen. And the same in India, where steam was synonymous with the nation itself, the end would never come. Whatever happened around the world there would always be steam trains in India. But by mid 1999 only one small section of main-line railway remained steam operated, the meter-gauge section between Wankener and Morvi in Gujarat, home to the last standard meter-gauge YG Mikados and YP Pacifics, popularly known in India as Black Beauties.

Witnessing those final runs brought memories flooding back to 1960s Britain where unkempt, run-down, filthy locomotives were eking out their last days on secondary workings. Outside the depot at Wankener lines of condemned engines stood in weed-covered yards while the laboured exhaust beats and banging bushes of the survivors echoed and reverberated around the town.

This was the end of an era on one of the great railway systems of the world, the end of a 150-year epoch and with the possible exception of Burma, the last passenger-hauling Pacifics on Earth. The Pacific was part of a golden age of express passenger locomotives and it will be remembered that the composer Artur Honegger paid tribute to the Pacific's fleet footedness in his composition 'Pacific 231'.

Fortunately, Wankener Depot was photogenic. The large amount of staff working there was completely out of proportion to the five locomotives that had to be turned out for daily traffic, although their run-down condition added much to the maintenance required. Wankener was a perfect microcosm of the great steam depots of yesterday; a fine team spirit prevailed and the depot foreman and footplate crews were supported by a team of artisans along with charge hands, boiler washers, ash-pit disposal gang, shed labourers and office staff.

The section between Wankener and Morvi was almost 19 miles long with four stations, three river bridges and a superb cutting at Vaghsay.

The long, cloudless days were a joy to work in and the slack the engines burnt made superb exhaust effects. Over several days I worked with Gaytriba Rana who modelled as 'Pot Girl' and we did some great pictures in the late afternoon sunlight at Vaghsay.

On one day in this enchanted place I saw a flock of at least a thousand Short-toed Larks. I also remember sitting by the lineside at Vaghsay, the sun beating down on my back, and realising that after leaving Wankener I would never again see a Pacific hauling a passenger train. It was an eerie, creeping realisation.

But quite apart from the sadness of steam ending in India, the two weeks I spent at Wankener in February and March 1999, were among the happiest days of my life. I was living in the maharajah's palace and my bedroom was in the building where the Duke of Connaught had lunch in 1887 while visiting India to commemorate Queen Victoria being proclaimed Empress of India. Meals were taken in the main palace with the maharajah's family. These included breakfast, lunch, a five-course evening dinner complete with Sheffield plate cutlery, afternoon tea and Bournvita at bedtime.

But there were also many other things to celebrate, my partner and my daughter, Marie-Louise, were with me. I had a vehicle and driver at my disposal, I was in perfect health, had money in my pocket and there were steam trains. Also I had one of the world's best cameras, a perfect climate in which to work, a wonderful model to appear in my pictures and a good supply of excellent cigars. The palace had a Steinway piano and the companionship of the maharajah and his family in the evenings was a crowning glory to those golden days.

Artisans to a man. The magnificent team of fitters who kept India's
last main-line steam locomotives running against all odds at Wankener
Depot in 1999 and into the year 2000. Their long experience and sheer
competence constituted skills that were to die with the locomotives

TOP LEFT Lady boiler washer Wankaner

BOTTOM LEFT Manual coaling with wicker baskets at Wankaner locomotive shed

LEFT One of the ashpit gangs at Wankaner locomotive shed with a YP Class Pacific in the background

LEFT Condemned meter gauge YG Mikados and YP Pacifics lie in the yard behind Wankaner Motive Power Depot

LEFT The ash-pit gang/shed labourers take a break to clean their teeth at Wankaner Motive Power Depot

TOP LEFT Tube cleaning Wankaner Motive Power Depot

ABOVE Clearing char from the smokebox of a YG Class 2-8-2

Ajmer Works, India

ON SATURDAY 13TH FEBRUARY 1999 I achieved a long-held ambition of visiting the historic railway works at Ajmer. There is always an excitement associated with visiting railway towns wherever they are in the world. Their historic industrial connections set them apart from and ahead of more ordinary places.

Formally the works of the Bombay Baroda and Central Indian Railway, Ajmer was the first to build meter-gauge locomotives in India in the form of the celebrated F Class 0-6-0s. Between 1895 and 1950, 467 new locomotives of many classes emerged from Ajmer Works. This was much higher than the total for the Eastern Railways' Jamalpur Works that produced 240 broad-gauge locomotives between 1885 and 1923.

Under British rule, most Indian locomotives were built in Britain and the Indian-built examples remained very much in the minority although they did have the effect of driving down the prices of British manufacturers. Ajmer produced some very distinctive designs of its own including 4-4-4Ts and 4-6-4Ts.

Sadly my visit was at the very end of steam and I was actually on route to Wankener to cover the line to Morvi that was the last section of Indian Railways to remain steam operated. The end was only months away and many standard, meter-gauge, YP and YG Pacific and Mikados were lying condemned in the works with just one engine, YG Class No.3437, being overhauled prior to returning to its home depot at Wankener. This engine was one of India's last steam build having come from the Tata Engineering and Locomotive Company Limited, Jamshedpur Bihar in 1962. This was almost certainly Ajmer's last steam overhaul.

The Victorian clock tower that presided over the plant set the scene for the entire works. The British presence could be felt intensely, the architecture and the layout of the offices and workshops were identical to those of Britain's railway towns in the age of steam.

My visit was on a Saturday so the works were not in operation and the silence served to heighten the atmosphere. As I walked the corridors and stairways I felt acutely conscious of following in the footsteps of generations of British engineers and administrators who had kept his once-vibrant place at the forefront of achievement under the Raj. This awareness engendered powerful emotions.

After photographing the YPs and YGs in the dismantling yard and No.3437 in the erecting shop, I left through the main gate at 17.30 believing that I would be the last Englishman to leave the shops at the end of a working day in the time of steam

LEFT Ajmer worksplate

RIGHT The dismantling yard at Ajmer works on the western railway on Saturday 13 February 1999. In the foreground is an Indian Railways' YP Class Pacific No.2795 (Telco1970) and in the background a YG Class Mikado No.3333 (Telco1960)

LEFT Ajmer works' Victorian clock with shops behind. The clock was manufactured in York by Cooke and Sons. Saturday 13th February 1999

New York Elevated Forneys, Alaska

ONE OF MY MOST MEMORABLE expeditions was to Alaska in June 2000 to document the former New York Elevated Forney 0-4-4Ts that lay abandoned in the mouth of the Solomon River. I was accompanied by Carol, my partner, Anteaus and Dominion, my twin sons, and Marie-Louise, my daughter.

After hours of flying over Alaska's snow-covered wilderness we were told to fasten our seat belts in readiness for landing in Nome. A century ago Nome became famous as the centre of the Gold Rush. After gold was discovered on the Seward Peninsular, thousands of adventurers set off to seek their fortune, invariably leaving families behind. Few found great riches and many perished in the ferocious Arctic winter.

Today Nome has about 3,500 inhabitants, many native Innuit. Nome can be reached only by air, the town's roads fizzle out in the surrounding hills and the nearest operating railway lies six hundred miles away in Anchorage.

We were greeted at the airport by Cussy Kauer, a descendent of one of the gold prospectors. We were staying with her and her husband Bob who was Nome's Chief of Police. As we drove into town she said: 'We've had heavy snow and haven't seen the sun for two weeks,' words that made the photographic task ahead more daunting.

Nome's main street looked like a scene from 'High Noon'. It was easy to imagine the turbulent years of the Gold Rush complete with saloons, dance halls and brothels. As we entered Cussy's well-appointed home, a huge polar bear towered above us on its hind legs. 'I hunted and shot that,' Cussy said coolly. That bear was to be a sauce of endless fascination to the twins throughout our stay.

I picked up the 4WD Discovery that was to be our expedition vehicle. There are no traffic lights in Nome, few vehicles and parking restrictions are unheard of. It had an air of relaxation and timelessness but with all the material comforts of western life on account of Alaska's economy being underwritten by the federal government.

For years I had dreamt about this expedition and now the Forneys lay only 35 miles to the east in the ghost town of Solomon. About three hundred Forneys worked on the extensive elevated suburban railways of New York

and Chicago during the 1880s/90s. They were noisy and smoky and the elevateds were electrified before the end of the century making the relatively new engines redundant.

Three of New York's engines built in the 1880s, were sold to the ill-starred Council City and Solomon River Railroad. Hastily built at the height of the Gold Rush, the line never reached Council City and when the bubble burst the engines were abandoned.

I had intended going up to Solomon the following day but by late afternoon the heavy clouds began to break up and shafts of sunlight rippled across the ground. Fearing that this could be the only sunlight seen, I set off immediately for Solomon. 'I don't know if they have opened the road yet following the snow,' Bob cautioned. 'Don't get the vehicle stuck, there will be no one up there to get you out.' I was apprehensive but, lighting a Petit Upmann cigar, I set off determined to reach Solomon.

It was a journey of extreme beauty. The rough road paralleled the Bering Sea. Massive snow drifts loomed up on either side and the ocean was covered in thick blocks of ice that rippled in the golden sunlight. By now the sky was clear transforming the sea into a deep aquamarine blue that appeared as a maze of exotic shapes in the pack ice. I rounded Cape Nome and ahead in the hazy blue distance was Cape Topkok, close to the mouth of the Solomon River. To my relief the road was passable and the first sight of the Forneys threw me into a trance. They lay slowly dissolving on the Arctic tundra in an amphitheatre of hills and were exactly where they had been left almost a hundred years previously.

I photographed avidly for four hours and it was almost midnight before I began the return journey to Nome. The sun would not set before 0200. The beauty and isolation of the Arctic landscape was overwhelming. The area abounded with wildlife, over two hundred bird species have been recorded from the peninsular and during that unforgettable drive a Short-eared Owl flew immediately alongside my vehicle for several miles, as if in some way I was being escorted.

I returned to Solomon every day over the next two weeks and photographed the Forneys in snow followed by flood as the thaw set in and when the thaw dried up, in brown tundra that was beginning to turn green by the end of the expedition. By August the engines would have been surrounded by yellow flowers, so rapid and dramatic are the climatic changes of the Arctic.

Every few days I sent film by the overnight plane for processing to Alaska's only Q-Lab in Anchorage. By arrangement they returned the films on the following day's plane, enabling me to monitor the photography. Had the Forneys been sculpted they could not have been in a more perfect setting, apart from the topography, the sun lit every part of them during its progression from sunrise to dusk. Combined with the seasonal variations and the immense historic significance of the locomotives, this is a unique site of scientific and industrial interest that is also one of the railway sights of the world.

On my return to Britain, I undertook a commission for Railtrack photographing the Croydon trams that are doing the same type of work as the Forneys were built to do. The two modes of photography reveal how two cities on opposite sides of the Atlantic Ocean and one and a quarter centuries apart, solved their urban transport problems. Such is the bliss and diversity of railway photography.

The three former New York Elevated Railway Forney 0-4-4Ts lie abandoned in the Alaskan wilderness. They have laid in the mouth of the Solomon River north of the Arctic Circle for over one hundred years and are so severely rusted that fragments of boiler tube dissolve between the fingers like wet cardboard

LEFT The Forney's cabs have fallen down and their bunkers capsized, having rusted through

Steam began on the New York Elevated Railways in 1871 and Forney Tank engines were the principal form of power over a network that eventually covered 280 route miles.

The three above Alaskan survivors are believed to be, leading: New York Locomotive Company, 1886, No.91 or 159, with Belpaire boiler. Middle: Baldwin No.5622 of 1881 numbered 103 with round top firebox and taper boiler, and at the rear, New York Locomotive Company, 1886, No.21 or 159 with Belpaire boiler.
It is worth recalling that these engines, along with the London Underground and the Chicago Elevated, operated the world's first inner-city trains

Beijing Limestone, China

A TAXI RIDE FROM THE TEAMING modernity of Beijing to the western suburb of Dahuichang revealed an operation that in an instant rolled back the centuries to the dawn of industry in the form of the Beijing Limestone Railway.

Here, four 28-tonne 0-8-0s of 762mm gauge hauled small four-wheeled tubs carrying limestone from the surrounding Lujia Hills to a huge processing plant that had the aura of an early iron foundry. The double-track system was a little under two miles in length and two locomotives were in operation at any one time.

After being dynamited, the limestone was loaded into the tubs through chutes in the roof of a tunnel in which the line ended. One locomotive hauled the empties to the tunnel mouth before detaching and reversing onto an adjacent line.

The wagons then went into the tunnel by electrically driven rope haulage. Once loaded, the engine coupled onto the rear wagon and drew the rake out as the second engine arrived with the next batch of empties.

The activity was rapid with trains running up and down every 15 to 20 minutes throughout the working day.

At the other end of the line the limestone was emptied into hoppers and sent to the works for processing. The finished product was then taken away by main-line, standard-gauge railway.

One of Beijing Limestone's 762mm-gauge 0-8-0s heads a rake of empties back to the loading tunnel. The processing works are in the background

A Chinese SY Class industrial
Mikado heads a loaded coal train
to the exchange with China
Railways on the Tieling Colliery
network in Liaoning Province.
The live slag tip in the rear of the
photograph is a characteristic
feature of this system.

China Coalfields

CHINA'S COALFIELDS are now the major source of surviving world steam. The country's booming economy and intense climatic contrasts have led to an insatiable demand for energy and the exploitation of many coalfields, both opencast and deep mined.

Many of the locomotives used in the mines are ex-China Railways in the form of JS Mikados or QJ 2-10-2s. These are ably backed and outnumbered by the industrial SY Class, American-inspired Mikados. Over 1,800 of this class were built, the last examples coming from Tangshan Works as recently as the mid 1990s.

The SYs evolution is fascinating because they are the type of locomotive that was prevalent on America's secondary roads almost a century ago.

China has many steam-worked collieries with new additions still being recorded. All have their own atmosphere and character.

Some remain 100 per cent steam, but creeping dieselisation is now inevitable. Some of these collieries are in a grimy industrial setting, others are relatively modern and inflict few scars on the landscape. At Tiefa in Liaoning Province a dense network of colliery lines was, until 2004, 100 per cent steam worked with SYs and a solitary JS. The system also had an inter-colliery workmen's passenger service. Tiefa was especially dramatic because huge slag tips from the workings dominated the landscape. These pyramid-like creations made a superb foil to the labouring steam trains, that when seen with the colliery's housing and winding gear, produced a form of industrial landscape that is almost non-existent today.

In nearby Nanpiao the hills are pock-marked with drift mines that are not rail connected and several large collieries that are. This is an exciting coalfield, full of atmosphere with slag tips and abandoned mines.

The area around Chifeng in Inner Mongolia also has steam-operated collieries. At Yuanbaoshan, collieries serve a huge power station and at Pingzhuang, the SYs can be seen operating in an opencast mine. I found operations at Manzhouli on the Russian border even more dramatic. It had an allocation of 25 SYs, with lines zigzagging down into a vast crater and the engines bringing up trains of spoil and coal. The lines are regularly slewed in order to follow the workings.

Some of my best coalfield adventures were at Pingdingshan in Henan Province in southeast China. The city is reached by way of a 13-hour overnight train journey from Beijing on trains that are punctual to the minute with a track-riding quality that is superb.

Pingdingshan Coal Company's roster included 20 steam locomotives made up of QJs, JSs, SYs and, at the time of my visit in July 2005, only two diesels.

Over a dozen collieries are in operation around Pingdingshan and all are rail connected. The system is busy and on average each colliery receives two return visits every shift.

The QJs diagrams are especially interesting as they serve a distant mine 37 miles away and operate four times a week with up to 70 loaded wagons with a QJ at either end, actions that would have been considered dramatic even at the height of the steam age.

The field produces soft coal that is used in power stations in the south of China.

The lines thread through a backdrop of slag tips and the inter-colliery tripping is reminiscent of the Nottinghamshire coalfield half a century ago, not least because of the workmen's passenger trains that are SY hauled and thread their way across the landscape, vividly recalling the Annesley Dido. It is as if Henry Priestley's wonderful pictures of the Nottinghamshire coalfield steam days had come alive again.

The railway's presence on Pingdingshan is exerted by the rhythmic clank of steam trains, sounds that are carried on the hot wind in summer and drift far across the surrounding countryside.

I remember one dramatic night during a spell of bad weather when a violent thunderstorm broke out. The rain cascaded down streets and turned them into rivers yet, above all the tumult and the flashes of intense lightning, the chime whistles of the locomotives was mixed with the crashing thunder and the driving rain as the coal trains went about their business unconcerned.

TOP LEFT Colliery winding gear with active slag tip - steam train passing

LEFT The Tieling colliery network's solitary JS Class Mikado heads a loaded train bound for the China Railways' connection

ABOVE A loaded coal train labours across the Teiling colliery system behind an SY Class industrial Mikado. January 2004

ABOVE A loaded coal train labours
across the Teiling colliery system
behind an SY Class industrial
Mikado. January 2004

RIGHT One of Yuanbaoshan's immaculate JS Class 2-8-2 passes a power station with a rake of coal from the open-cast mine. December 2005

RIGHT JS Class No.8068 arrives at Colliery No.4 on the Pingdingshan coal system in Henan Province on Friday 15th July 2005

LEFT Linghai Colliery No.1, abandoned

ABOVE Yuanbaoshan's allocated JS Class No.8216 in Colliery No.2 on Tuesday 13th December 2005

LEFT Wanbao mine near Zhaojiatun on the Nanpiao coalfield. Wednesday 2nd March 2005

ABOVE Loco shed detail, Nanpiao,
Monday 14th March 2005

RIGHT Track layout detail at Xi
yard on theYuanbaoshan colliery
network, Inner Mongolia. Tuesday
13th December 2005

Steam's Last Great Fling, Ji-Tong Railway, Inner Mongolia

OUR MINI BUS JUMPED and gyrated over an un-made stretch of road on the approach to Jing Peng. I was with Carol, my partner, Marie-Louise, my daughter and Antaeus and Dominion, our four-year-old twin boys. Also onboard was Bao Dan Dan, a 23-year-old Mongolian girl as beautiful as she was personable, who was our guide for the expedition. Our driver was Qi Bao Feng who, we were to find out, was prepared to take his vehicle almost anywhere in the name of railway photography. These were to be our companions over the coming three weeks as we disappeared into the Da Hinggang Mountains, back to the age of steam. Our target was the Ji-Tong Railway that connects the industrial cities of Jining in the west and Tongliao in the east. Well over six hundred miles long, the line was built in the early 1990s, opened in December 1995 and was 100 per cent steam worked. At Jing Peng in the east and Reshui in the west the railway begins its climb through a mountain range. The summit lies in a tunnel in the middle of the mountains and is approached by a climb of 15 miles on either side. It is a section of railway known as the Jing-Peng Pass.

As we entered Jing Peng, snowflakes swirled in the wind. The temperature was a mere two degrees centigrade, normally it would have been -20. We were heading for Reshui, a small town at the opposite end of the mountain section where we were to make our base at the Railway Hotel. As we drove out towards the snow-covered mountains, the railway came into view and further up the valley we saw a freight train, the engines blasting their way up the mountainside with massive smoke columns rising into the air. 'QJs' shouted the twins, (they had seen many pictures of them). We caught up with the train up at Guangtaike as it snaked around a loop at the head of the valley and started to curve back down the other side. It would then cross the massive horseshoe viaduct at Simingyi before swinging sharply away into Tunnel No.1.

We stopped at the viaduct to watch the train pass. The QJs flung themselves at the gradient, the deep throbbing coughs of their exhausts reverberating around the hills, the rhythms intensifying whenever one of the engines slipped a little. With a deafening roar the giants reached the viaduct with their massive coal train that was complete with a guard's van at the end. With the train engine enveloped in a pall of steam, they forged past us and rounded the hillside and with whistles screaming they plunged into the tunnel. In an instant silence fell, apart from the gentle rumble of wagons, However, a massive mushroom of smoke spiralled skywards out of the tunnel mouth. On emerging from the tunnel, the engine's exhaust echoed through the mountains and a black, sooty smoke pall towered above the peaks. I glanced at the twins' faces, they were literally wide-eyed and open-mouthed at the incredible audio-visual spectacle they had just witnessed. Here, at the age of four, was their first experience of the age of steam, a memory they will carry for life.

We reached the hotel in Reshui at dusk, it was owned by the Ji-Tong Railway and the forecourt contained a large, heroic statue of a female holding aloft the company's symbol. Our room overlooked the line and that night we fell asleep to the sound of trains leaving the loop at Reshui to begin the climb. The engine's gorgeous chime whistles resonated through the bitter night air with superb clarity. This was the railway equivalent of Jurassic Park, here in this remote part of the world we had found the valley of the dinosaurs. It was incredible that this last line should be as magnificent as any experienced in the heyday of steam. I am tempted to compare the Jing Peng with the legendary Sherman Hill and its Union Pacific Railways' 'Big Boy' 4-8-8-4s. I remember the awe I felt on talking recently to a veteran American cameraman who had photographed every 'Big Boy' attacking Sherman Hill.

And yet the Jing Peng was not an easy line to photograph. The short winter days gave only about eight trains in daylight and the twisting curvature of the line led to irascible lighting so that some of the classic views were properly lit only for an hour or so at a time. Even greater problems were created by the wind that played havoc with the engine's exhaust and frequently a train would fall into the shadow of its own smoke. Often a superb composition was totally destroyed by the smoke blowing down and obliterating both engines or, conversely, a picture orientated around distant peaks would be lost when all the peaks disappeared behind a cloud of exhaust. Another hazard, ever present, was the bitter climate that gave one a physical hammering, particularly when at the lineside for hours on end. If the vehicle were near by it was possible to recuperate between trains but if I had hiked up into the hills there was no such back up.

As brilliant as Canon EOS cameras are, they cannot be set up and operated when wearing gloves, but discarding them even for one minute would cause a vicious attack on one's fingers, leaving them almost useless or at worse incapable of pressing the shutter, all feeling in the hand having disappeared. I found that on days when the temperature was inching towards -25C mental disorientation set in, like the draining of a battery, and even the simplest of decisions became difficult to make. But it was the stuff of adventure, the days were completely full of excitement.

Here is a random extract taken from my diary dated 16th December 2003: 'Power off this morning; dressed by candlelight, it took 40 minutes – seven layers of clothing. I emerged from the hotel at dawn to find Qi Bao Feng sitting in the mini bus with the engine running. It was an overcast, foggy day with fierce gusts of wind that forced a programme change. Instead of going to the summit at Shangdian I walked the hills above Reshui in search of the loop but failed to find it. An enormous gale blew me down the railway embankment once and almost off the hillside half an hour later. Snow threatens but hasn't fallen. Concerned about the inclement weather, valuable time is being lost. Minus 25 degrees Celsius and still cloudy so we moved west through the pass to explore the villages on either side of the station.

'I found several themes including a set grid below an embankment with pigs and cows visible along the village street. Very few people around today, everyone in their homes shuttered up against the weather.

'The family went shopping in Jing Peng and found wonderful fruits, cereals, coffee, milk and biscuits along with two tins of baked beans for the twins. I will get the kitchen to prepare them for their dinner tonight. We returned early to the hotel and I spent the evening editing yesterday's pictures on the lap top.

'No photography was done today but I am thrilled by the stark village scenes we found in Xiakengzi and intend to head back there first thing tomorrow – it will almost certainly be sunny.'

The landscape was in a constant state of change. The heavy wind stripped the exposed mountain faces of snow and deposited it elsewhere, so careful planning was needed to feature snow in the landscape. The exposed rock had a wonderful golden colour in the sunlight. The rugged landscape and the bleak villages have a wild beauty that is utterly captivating. I found great fulfilment in the terrain as well as the trains. The late afternoons in Xiakengzi were especially beautiful, trains were audible for almost 30 minutes soon after leaving Jing Peng until they were almost at the summit. A massive pall of black smoke hung high above the mountains for 20 minutes after the trains had passed. The QJs would blow down frequently and shoot gallons of scalding water and thunderous clouds of steam at the defiant mountains.

The Ji-Tong Railway attracted photographers from all over the world, also in Reshui were a party of Germans and a lone Japanese who looked as if he had walked straight out of a Burt Lancaster World War Two movie. He would have been perfectly cast as a concentration-camp adjutant with his impassioned manner and intense eyes. He talked in rapid, broken English about the Tiefa coalfield that was our next target, and he spread an enormous map across the dining table, quite oblivious of the waitresses waiting to serve food, and jabbed his finger enthusiastically at the location of the slag tips that abound around Tiefa.

Having known people who suffered in the far-eastern theatre in World War Two, I appreciated the fact that we were meeting in the name of railway photography.

On Christmas night we all joined together for a party, Germans, our Japanese friend and a Swede who had turned up in the meantime. Cigars were smoked and one of the Germans, a banker from Stuttgart, plugged his video camera into the TV and we all relived the day's action. Also at the hotel were a group of officials from the Ji-Tong Railway and, in the Mongolian tradition, they greeted us by each singing a song. This charming custom was tempered somewhat when it became apparent that we were expected to return the compliment.

It was a very happy expedition, Marie-Louise developed a rapid friendship with Bao Dan Dan and shared her room. Qi Bao Feng with his rugged determination, was the perfect driver and also was a great help with the twins, especially at meal times when he would gently coerce them to try some of the more unusual dishes.

Our days on the Ji-Tong were some of the most rewarding of my life. I realised once again that the allure of the steam age is not misplaced nostalgia, it really was as fabulous as we remember it.

How long steam will survive on this unbelievable railway is the question on the lips of tens of thousands of railway photographers and enthusiasts the world over. The railway management have proved that steam is marginally cheaper than converting to diesel and they would be happy to continue with the QJs, but central government is now exerting pressure to be rid of steam in order for China to improve its image as a modern nation.

Apparently, all steam must be gone throughout China by 2008 when Beijing hosts the Olympics. In the early months of 2005 the Jitong was fully dieselised. And so main line steam will pass into the sands of time just over two hundred years after the steam locomotives birth in a Welsh ironworks.

A westbound freight heads across the viaduct at Reshui on a late afternoon in December 2004

The morning sun haloes an eastbound freight as it fights the gradient up from Billigou to Xiakengzi

Biligou Viaduct was magnificent in its structure and environment but I found it very difficult to photograph satisfactorily, its distinctiveness was elusive. I had almost written it out of the script until this freshly ploughed field provided a new aspect and one that enabled me to express everything I wanted to say

Nandian, Ji-Tong Railway, Inner Mongolia

THIS DELIGHTFUL VILLAGE lies alongside the railway on the approach to the summit tunnel from the east. From the far end of the village it was possible to look back to the railway and include the village in the foreground, 'Animal Fold' and 'Water Girl' being two such scenes. The same woman modelled for both pictures and there are also some classic takes of her walking her cow along the snow-covered village main street. I loved the atmosphere of Nandian and worked there over both expeditions with Liu Yanchun. I knew it only in winter but its bleakness stood out better then and

large palls of exhaust were necessary to emphasise the train's presence in the background.

We had the sanctity of our model's warm house to escape the bitter winter wind that coursed through the village. Leaving the camera set up on its tripod, we could escape for drinks of hot tea, convivial company and an opportunity to smoke a cigar.

We must have visited the village a dozen times, not least because the prevailing wind from the west often blew the smoke down over the train and on occasions obliterated it completely.

Guangtaihe lies between Biligou viaduct and Simingyi viaduct. It was one of my favourite locations on the Jingpeng pass and its bleakness is emphasised in this late morning scene of two QJs toiling up the grade from Xikengzi

ABOVE 'Water Girl', one of my favourite themes from the Jing Peng expeditions. The picture expresses the starkness of these beautiful villages and the partly obscured engines evoke the genre of the 'distant passing trains' as expressed by the watercolourist David Cox

RIGHT A fall of snow during the early hours of Sunday 19th December 2004 enabled this companion picture to 'Water Girl' to be made.

TOP RIGHT My favourite picture from Nandian is 'Animal Fold'.

RIGHT Summit Tunnel lies just to the west of Nandian village and making these pictures was both frightening and unforgettable

Er-Di, Ji-Tong Railway, Inner Mongolia

THIS VILLAGE was one of the most exciting locations on the Jing Peng Pass. There were four classic pictures to be made within a short walk from its main street. Just beyond the village the line curved from one side of the valley to the other crossing a viaduct in the process. Known as Brickwork's Viaduct this was the location for a classic picture of eastbound trains taken in the morning from the hillside looking down on the viaduct, but never before 09.00 as the winter sun had not risen above the mountains until then.

Immediately after crossing the viaduct the trains entered Tunnel No.2 and emerged half way up the mountain overlooking the village. By climbing this mountain to the rocky defiles that overlooked the railway, it was possible to watch the train crossing Brickwork's Viaduct and to see the engine emerge from the tunnel before the guard's van disappeared from view on the viaduct.

Late afternoon studies at Er-di were very sensual. When the village street became shrouded half in sunlight and half in shadow, the starkness of the dwellings was emphasized and the eastbound trains crossing the viaduct were lit by the afternoon sun on the other side. Other superb pictures were obtained from the opposite side of the valley, again after a steep climb up the mountain to look down on the railway. By looking back westwards towards Hadashan, superb pictures of the climbing trains could be made with Hadashan village in the background.

OPPOSITE PAGE Village scene near Er-Di

LEFT A side street in Er-Di. The passing train in this afternoon scene has just crossed Brickwork's Viaduct and is about to enter the tunnel

The main street in Er-Di complete with afternoon shadows. The train has just crossed Brickwork's Viaduct and is about to enter the tunnel. This picture, dated Friday 17th December 2004, shows a diesel pilot; the run down of steam having begun

An eastbound freight climbs
towards Brickwork's Viaduct with
Hadashan village in the
background

Brickwork's Viaduct in superb
morning light. The eastern end of
Er-Di village lies just behind the
embankment on the right

Semaphore signals at Xiakengzi with an eastbound freight approaching

RIGHT An eastbound freight climbs the embankment above Xiakengzi on the approach to the station with the village in the foreground

Xiakengzi, Ji-Tong Railway, Inner Mongolia

THIS WAS THE FIRST CROSSING loop for trains heading eastwards from Jing Peng. The line was on a high embankment above the village and so to get the trains in the background I chose many locations on the main street with its profusion of cows, foraging pigs and noisy chickens.

The occupants of the angular brick houses added additional interest on foot, on cycles, pushing handcarts or carrying shoulder yokes, all part of the colourful tapestry of village life. But my favourite picture at Xiakengzi was 'Animal Wall'. There horses, donkeys and cows were tethered in a partially enclosed area of rough ground. Behind and up above was the main line and as the QJs toiled towards the camera, the animals made a superb foil. I did many variations of Animal Wall although on a number of occasions there were no animals present.

The best take of all was during a heavy snow storm. The train is just visible and contrasts superbly with the bleak angular houses silhouetted against the snow-covered embankment. Unfortunately there were no animals present but the violent weather added its own animation to the picture.

This morning view of Xiakengzi
was one of the most difficult
pictures. It demanded snow and a
perfectly still day as any hint of
the prevailing wind would blow
the exhaust down over the train

An eastbound freight fights its
way up to Xiakengzi during a
blizzard

LEFT 'Animal Wall', with eastbound freight approaching the semaphores

BOTTOM The main street at Xiakengzi with an eastbound freight approaching the semaphores

ABOVE A west bound freight waits
at Xiakengzi for a climbing
eastbound train to pass

Guangtaihe, Ji-Tong Railway, Inner Mongolia

TWO MILES EAST OF XIAKENGZi was the lineside village of Guangtaihe; it was located at the point were the railway swings across the valley and proceeds back down the other side towards Simigyi Viaduct before sharply diverging into the mountains through Tunnel No.1. A track, leading from the village to the road, ran parallel to the railway and the main theme here was to get donkey carts with the passing trains. One of the best takes ever achieved was of a villager solitarily leading his donkey along the path; forlorn and hunched against the cold as a brace of QJs storm eastwards. Like Xiakengzi, Guangtaihe had a marvellous atmosphere and in the village was a boiler with a chimney on top. it was a strange, angular structure; it matched the bleakness of the buildings and made an ideal foreground to the walled houses with a train approaching in the far distance from Xiakengzi.

Three other themes were selected at Guangtaihe, firstly, several donkeys spent most of their leisure time tethered around a cart and made a superb foreground for the westbound trains coming down the bank; secondly, the wide frozen river which passes under the viaduct was a perfect arena for skaters and colourful children playing on the ice in low afternoon light made a wonderful foreground to the passing trains. And thirdly, just before the sun dipped below the mountains in the afternoon, its reflection gold plated the sides of the eastbound trains; an effect which was particularly scintillating in the snowy surroundings.

LEFT The late afternoon sun highlights an east bound freight passing Guangtaihe. The bleakness of the village and outlying animal folds heighten the atmosphere of this desolate place

RIGHT A donkey cart plods its way over the frozen earth at Guangtaihe as two QJs pass with an eastbound freight

Contrasting modes of transport at
Guangtaihe

A brace of QJs hammer an east bound freight through Guangtaihe in the classic manner. Scenes such as this are now gone forever

Simingyi, Ji-Tong Railway, Inner Mongolia

THE CURVED CONCRETE viaduct at Simingyi became the symbol of the Jing Peng Pass and the QJs made a superb spectacle as they crossed over it. The best time for pictures at Simingyi was around 16.00 when the golden sunlight of late afternoon coloured the viaduct with a warm glow. Often there was no eastbound train at this time or, on days that there was, the wind may be blowing the exhaust down too low. On a still afternoon the exhaust usually went high enough into the sky. But even this wasn't the ultimate as, ideally, the mountains behind the viaduct would be snow covered - a very rare occurrence and one which eluded me on all three expeditions as a fall of snow on those particular mountains was quickly blown off by the prevailing wind. The viaduct was visible from afar and from most points of the compass and was an endlessly fascinating subject to photograph.

The sheer magic of the Jing Peng Pass section of the Ji-Tong Railway is shown in this view of Simigyi Viaduct. The east bound freight, seen approaching, will curve round and over the viaduct at Guangtaihe to come back on the near side of the valley and cross the viaduct from right to left before entering Tunnel No.1.

An eastbound freight, having
crossed the viaduct at
Guangtaihe, curves round the
opposite side of the valley soon to
cross the viaduct at Simingyi. The
Chinese characters in the left
foreground say 'Keep the forest
free of fire'

The magnificent curved viaduct at
Simingyi

LEFT An eastbound freight crosses the viaduct with Guangtaihe village visible in the top right hand corner

LEFT An eastbound freight, having crossed Simingyi Viaduct, prepares to enter Tunnel No.1

West of Hadashan: In the last weeks of steam a diesel pilot assists an eastbound freight. The train is seen emerging from Tunnel No.1. Simingyi Viaduct that the train has just crossed, is visible in the background. The picture is dated Saturday 18th December 2004

Tunnel No.4, Ji-Tong Railway, Inner Mongolia

'Imagine dreaming that in the wilds of Inner Mongolia hidden from the rest of the world, is a new railway, 589 miles long and worked 100 per cent by steam. And the route has double-headed 2-10-2s dragging 2,300-tonne trains, climbing through a mountain range with 1-in-80 gradients, the line abounding in spirals, viaducts and tunnels and so dramatically engineered that one could make pictures as fine as any taken in the 200-year history of steam locomotives. And the line, signalled by attractive semaphores, was totally accessible. One could walk the track and take pictures from any vantage point one wished, there were no restrictions. Imagine waking up after a dream like that, imagine how crestfallen one would be on realising that it was but a dream. But this time the dream was real....'

THE JI-TONG RAILWAY in Inner Mongolia was the last major steam line in the world, it ran from Jining in the west to Tongliao in the east and the 30-mile section through the Da Hinggang mountains was a spectacular feat of construction. During the harsh Mongolian winter the temperature drops to -25 degrees centigrade. This means extreme discomfort when by the lineside but did ensure the most amazing exhaust effects from the locomotives. And there were photographic locations wherever one looked, I had never experienced so photogenic a stretch of railway. Trains from the east and west climbed steeply to the summit that was located in the middle of Tunnel No.3, halfway through the mountain range.

I spent ten weeks of concentrated photography on that 30-mile stretch of railway over three expeditions between 2003 and 2005. I got to know the major photographic locations intimately and my favourite was Tunnel No.4. The area around its hallowed portals at the eastern end could only be described as organic. There was a whole range of spectacular morning pictures to be made from the mountain that overlooked the tunnel from the eastern side featuring the climbing trains as they emerged from the tunnel. In the afternoon pictures could be made not just from the mountains on the opposite side of the line – the sun having moved over – but a whole range of

expressions of animals and shepherds along with the homesteads of an adjacent village.

The morning view from the east side was as dramatic a railway picture as I have ever seen. But one had to be up at the location ready for the reveal – when the winter sun rises high enough above the mountains to illuminate the line. Depending on the month this occurs between 8.30 and 9.00. Although on most days there were clear skies, the prevailing north-westerly wind invariably would blow the smoke down over the train, completely invalidating the picture. It was on the rare, still mornings that the magic of Tunnel No.4 revealed itself. Even on days that dawned without a breath of wind, luck played a big part. There was often a three-hour gap between trains and by 11.00 the light had gone over too far.

The definitive challenge was to get a climbing train between 8.30 and 9.30 on a sunny, windless day. How often had I been on location only to find the wind had got up by 9.00. And the climb wasn't easy, it was a 40-minute slog from the nearest road, up through fields, over the railway and up the steep mountain. It was a climb that I had done at least 20 times and still had not made the definitive picture. It was grim, barefaced determination that took me back to that enchanted place morning after morning.

I must recount a true story about Tunnel No.4. The day had dawned windless and clear after a fall of snow overnight. I set out to climb to my designated point. It was 8.45 and I was only halfway up the mountain, the snow having delayed me. The reveal had already occurred but I fought my way up slipping and sliding back on the loose, icy stones and using my tripod as a climbing iron. As I forged my way up the mountain, dragging my camera case behind me, I distinctly heard the reverberating exhaust beat of two QJs climbing up towards the tunnel. There was at least ten minutes of climbing ahead of me and I knew I might never get another opportunity on a day like this, windless, clear and a wonderful fall of snow. I redoubled my efforts, literally throwing myself at the mountain; my breath came in short, sharp stabs. The more I struggled the nearer the sounds came. A sinking feeling of abject dismay came over me. I was not going to make it and would be remonstrating with myself for days afterwards over a missed opportunity.

The hollow, pounding throbs of the train came ever closer but it was no good, I had to take a rest and allowed myself to stumble, face down onto the rocks where I lay gasping for breath. I listened to the rhythm of the train for a few seconds before an awesome realisation dawned on me. There were no QJs climbing the mountain, the sounds I had heard were the poundings of my heart that, partly disguised by the sound of falling stones, had sounded exactly like the hollow exhaust beat of a brace of QJs.

LEFT The sheer magic of Tunnel No.4 is captured in this early-morning drama

ABOVE An eastbound mixed freight emerges from Tunnel No.4 and hammers its way up the gruelling incline towards Shangdian

RIGHT The afternoon aspect of Tunnel No.4 was also enthralling, here a pair of QJs at the head of an eastbound freight, leave wraithes of steam oozing from the tunnel mouth

FAR RIGHT Early morning above Tunnel No.4 as an eastbound freight raises the echoes with the amazing shape of Mount Hadashan in the background

Shangdian, Ji-Tong Railway, Inner Mongolia

IMUST HAVE WALKED down to the distant semaphore signal on the western approach to Shangdian station on at least 20 occasions. The gradient profile past the signal was especially steep and every take was different on account of the weather conditions, the direction of the wind, embellishments on the locomotive, the colour and density of the exhaust and the amount of snow in the landscape, if any.

Another favourite position for photographing this final lap to the summit was off the top of a high field alongside the station. This had the advantage of catching the blow down as both engines on the climbing trains often blew down shortly before entering the station. I remember one bitterly cold day when a terrible wind was blowing, it was at least -25 degrees Centigrade and with Liu Yanchun I stood on the high field for four hours waiting for an eastbound freight.

When it finally came it looked magnificent despite the weather, the drabness of the day added drama. We watched the QJs pass the distant semaphore and come through the short cutting.

As the train came into shooting range, both engines blew down simultaneously. It was a fantastic moment and well worth every second of the agonising wait.

But the greatest good fortune occurred in 2004 when driving down to Xiakengzi with Liu Yanchun. We noticed a train stalled near Simingyi Viaduct, presumably one of the engines had failed. I realised that the pilot from the next train would be detached at Xiakengzi and would run up to the crippled train and bank it to the summit.

We turned around immediately and drove back to Shangdian and I hurried down to the distant semaphore. From here the track was straight and if a banker were on it would be visible. There was no tradition of banking on the Jing Peng Pass.

I waited over an hour and no train came, and neither could one go down from Shangdian of course, the stricken train having blocked the line. And then I heard the sound of a climbing train, was it being banked?

I held my breath, the light was perfect. The train came into sight and there, to my surging joy, was a banker, sending up a huge plume of white steam high into the air at the rear of the train. The resulting picture was everything I could have hoped for and, arguably, was as good as anything achieved on three expeditions to the fabled Jing Peng Pass.

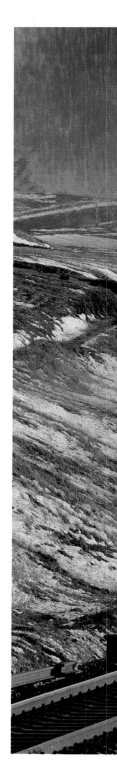

An eastbound freight whistles up for departure from Shangdian. Shortly it will enter the western portal of Summit Tunnel and drift down the bank past Nandian to Reshui at the eastern end of the pass

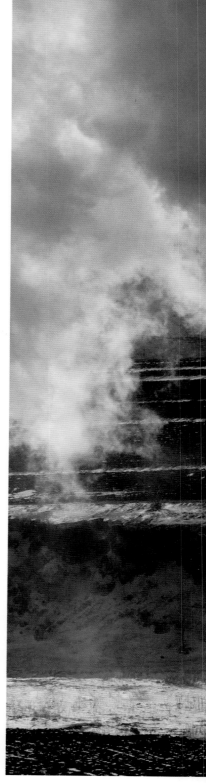

ABOVE The distant signal for Shangdian is 'off' for the approaching eastbound freight. Pictorial variations at this fabulous location took me there on at least 20 occasions

RIGHT One of those occasions was the morning a QJ failed at Simingyi. The pilot of the following train had to bank the cripple up to the summit at Shangdian. This was the only time I experienced a banker on the Jing Peng Pass

This picture was achieved after standing for hours on a windswept
hillside near Shangdian in temperatures of -25 degrees Centigrade.
Both engines are blowing down, the horizontal jets of steam lining up
with the twisted exhausts blown by the fierce gusts of wind

FAR LEFT An eastbound freight catches the sun's final minutes on the approach to Shangdian summit. Shangdian village, in all its wintry attire, lies in deep shadow in the foreground

LEFT A snowy, cloudy day on the Jing Peng Pass as an eastbound freight toils up the severe gradient to Shangdian